The Courage to Love

By Kedarji

The Bhakta School of Transformation, Inc.
Youngstown, Ohio

The Courage to Love

By Kedarji

Copies of this book may be ordered through booksellers or by contacting:

The Bhakta School of Transformation, Inc.
330-623-7388 Ext 10

NityanandaShaktipatYoga.org

ISBN: 979-8-218-50940-8

Printed in the United States of America

Contents

Introduction

By Your Love I Am

Where You Are I Am

Where I Am You Are

In Flowers, Trees, Grass and Water I Am

In Roots and Fibers and Dirt and Wind I Am

When You See, I Am What Is Seen

When I See, You Are What Is Seen

By Your Love I Am Omniscient, Omnipotent and Omnipresent

Sun and Moon Am I

Tracing My Own Steps Across the Sky

Appearing and Disappearing In a Single Breath

Welling Up In Space and Time

By Your Grace, I Am the Revealer and the Revealed

Residing In Being Be

All That Is Comes to Complete Rest In Me

My Devotion to You Has Turned Me From a
Beggar to a King

By Your Love I Am

What Is Love?

In his Bhakti Sutras, the great sage Narada defines Love in the following way: "When Love comes, God reveals himself. By attaining it, a person becomes perfect, immortal and satisfied forever. This is how you know that it is Love."

When I first read this utterance, I found it hard to accept in any way. At that time, my understanding of Love came mostly from being infatuated with others. I did not understand the difference between Love and being 'in love.' I knew nothing of the difference between infatuation and Love. There is a difference.

"What is love? Baby don't hurt me, don't hurt me, no more"
~ *Hit dance song by Haddaway*

At that time in my existence, my understanding of Love was entirely based on the degree to which I was able to successfully engage in the bartering and trading of needs for wants. The degree to which I felt *in control* in this trading, along with whether or not I felt there was equality in this bartering/trading between myself and others determined, in my view, the degree to which I was 'successful' in love. Sound familiar?

In addition, all of my understandings about Love and how to attain it came from my parents, close friends and authority figures in my life. I modeled after those who I felt were more 'successful' in love than me.

My understanding and experience of Love became skewed with each breakup. I became guarded and manipulative. Trust grew to be something foreign to me and, gradually, it came to represent a loss of control. With this perception came a decline in compassion and a bitterness with respect to intimacy. Lovers became mere objects of desire and friends had to meet my 'what have you done for me lately' standard. This predicament went on for quite some time. Then, by God's Grace, I met my Guru.

King Bartruhari

There was a great king named Bartruhari. He was a great warrior and also a kind, benevolent ruler. Bartruhari was loved by the people of the kingdom he ruled.

One day a monk went to the palace to see the king. Bartruhari received him with gratitude for his visit. The monk then presented the king with a rare fruit and told the king that, if he ate the fruit, it would make him young and immortal, that he would live forever in his body.

King Bartruhari accepted the fruit. After the monk left his court, Bartruhari thought, "I am not worthy of this fruit. I should give this fruit to my queen, my great love, so that she can remain young and immortal to serve me and love me for the rest of my days." So, the king went to his wife's quarters and presented her with the fruit. He exclaimed how much he loved her and explained how eating the fruit would make her young and immortal. The queen accepted the fruit but told the king that she had been gardening. She wanted to bath first and said that she would eat the fruit later, after she cleaned up.

Once the king had left her bedchamber, his wife thought, "I am not the one for this fruit. It should be given to my lover so that he will stay with me and love me for all of my days. She took the fruit and rushed to the horse stables. She was having an affair with the stable boy and found him minding the horses. She professed her love for him and told him about the fruit and its qualities. Then she handed him the fruit and told him to eat it in her presence. The boy told the queen, "Thank you. I will certainly eat this fruit so that I can remain young and immortal to forever love you. But I am so dirty from washing the horses. Let me bath first and then I will eat the fruit." So, the queen returned to the palace.

The stable boy then thought, "I am not worthy of this fruit. I will give it to my lover so that she can remain ever young and immortal to love me for all of my days." Then he rushed to the local brothel where his lover, a prostitute, was working her shift. He interrupted her to offer her the fruit, explaining its qualities and telling her how much he loved her and wanted her to have it. She told him, "Look. I am in the middle of my shift. I have a John scheduled right now. Let me finish work and then I will come to you and eat the fruit." The stable boy agreed and returned to the palace stables.

Staring at the fruit, the prostitute thought, "I am unworthy of such a gift. There is only one person worthy of this gift of youth and immortality. Our king is such a kind, benevolent king. He is a great ruler. He should have this fruit so that he can remain young and immortal to

rule over our kingdom forever." The woman
rushed to the palace with the fruit and requested
to see King Bartruhari.

The king was seated, holding court and
agreed to hear the prostitute. The prostitute
bowed to the king and then presented him with
the fruit, explaining its qualities. "Only you, O
king, are deserving of such a gift." Of course, the
king immediately recognized the fruit. He then
said, "Fie on all that which masquerades as Love.
Let me meditate on the Self and Love God!" The
king then took a Guru and began to engage the
wisdom and practices that delivered him to the
experience of Supreme Love.

Supreme Love

Love is a necessity for our existence. We
cannot survive without Love. And any form and
degree of Love is better than no Love at all.
However, this can only be understood in the
context of what Love really is. For, Love is
Supreme and there is nothing higher, nothing
greater than Love. I only began to understand
this by keeping the company of my Guru,
Muktananda Paramahamsa. By His Love I am. By
His Love I came to understand and experience
God's Love for me and for all sentient and
insentient beings. By His Grace I came to know
what Love really is and began to revel in its
overwhelming power.

For Love to be Love it cannot be
conditional. It cannot be dependent on anything
or anyone outside yourself because that would
make it conditional. A physician once said,

"The best medicine is Love." Someone asked, "What if it doesn't work?" He smiled and answered, "Increase the dose."

God exists in everything and everyone, everywhere. My Guru always said, "See God in each other." He also said, "Kneel to yourself. Bow to yourself. God dwells within you as you." God is an endless ocean of Love. Love is the greatest power in our existence. Out of Love the Sun rises and sets. Out of Love the moon waxes and wanes. It is Love that causes grass, trees, plants and flowers to grow. Due to Love we have so many animals, creepers and insects in this Earth plane. It is why Earth is also known as the Love planet.

By Love alone we are able to conquer fear. In fact, Love is all there is. By Love we are able to realize the highest, our God nature. It is Love that allows us to experience Joy. We come to treasure each other by Love. By Love we breath. It is Love that gives us sight. Love allows us to hear and feel. By Love we are able to walk, run, leap, listen, sleep, awake and revel in life. For these reasons the recognition of Love is so necessary. Without Love we don't exist.

What Makes Love Supreme?

No conditions is what makes Love Supreme. The experience of the indescribable Joy of the Self is what makes Love Supreme. By this Joy a person is transformed by leaving off the false notion of individuality to experience Oneness with God.

"The Heart is the hub of all sacred places. Go there and roam."
~ *Bhagawan Nityananda of Ganeshpuri*

Jalal al-Din Rumi was a Persian Sufi mystic whose writings have become popular all over the world. Rumi's Guru was Shams of Tabreze who was a disciple of Baba Kamal al-Din Jumdi. The writings of Sri Rumi evoke the Love of the true heart. One of my favorite utterances of Rumi is "Your task is not to seek for love, but merely to seek and find all the barriers within yourself that you have built against it." This utterance tells the story of how so many confuse satisfaction for Love.

Here Rumi also speaks of the act of concealment. The barriers represent all the ways in which Love is concealed *by way of protecting fear and the useless notions that manifest as a result.* Growing up and well into adulthood I was taught that I had to find someone to be with, someone who could 'complete me.' This notion is also known as that of the 'soulmate.'

I observed that everyone in my life, including my parents, other family members, friends, associates and lovers lived in fear of being alone or in fear of being abandoned. Then I also observed in them the fear of not having, of not getting what was wanted, the fear of loss and FOMO, the fear of missing out. Fear, fear, fear. Since such people in my life were in the majority at the time, I took on these qualities by way of embracing the understandings that they embraced. I felt that by doing so I was improving my lot in life.

However, as a result, I found myself living in a state of doubt, worry and anxiety. Rather than increasing my desire to know what Love really is, this only increased my pursuit of satisfaction. I had built a fantasy about love on a model that could never lead to the experience of what Love is. I tied this fantasy to my limiting desires and cravings and the expectation of outcomes connected to these. More fear followed.

Then I began to reflect on my Guru's instruction to contemplate the utterances of Shri Narada in the Narada Bhakti Sutras – beginning with "When Love comes, God reveals himself. By attaining it, a person becomes perfect, immortal and satisfied forever. This is how you know that it is Love."

"When Love comes, God reveals himself."

In the experience of Love, God is revealed. It is now my experience that God is Love. In the direct experience of the inner Self, the highest nature of living beings, there is Joy. This Joy, also referred to as Bliss, is the direct experience of God and the direct experience of Love. In this experience of Love, we are fully present with God. Therefore, when this experience is absent, that cannot be Love. It is as Narada says: to be Love there must be the experience of the Joy, the Bliss of the true heart that is God. Indeed, this is a simple, immediate and most reliable way to know whether we are experiencing Love or not.

"By attaining it, a person becomes perfect, immortal and satisfied forever. This is how you know that it is Love."

Becoming *perfect* is a matter of expanding your knowledge of the Self, God, by way of the expansion of your experience of the indescribable Joy of the Self. Perfection is being fully present with your God nature in this way, from moment to moment, as you go about your daily mundane activities. This experience of the Bliss of the Self, over time, leads to the experience of Happiness. Happiness is a spiritual principle that is not dependent on anything or anyone outside yourself. Happiness is the death of satisfaction that occurs as you drown in the ocean of Love. This is perfection and this perfection comes by way of practicing the methods for increasing your direct experience of indescribable Joy.

Immortality is the direct experience that you are God, the Self, that Indweller who is the witness to your mind and all your thoughts. As your experience of the indescribable Joy of the Self increases, you begin to realize that you are not the mind, the body or the senses. You begin to realize that you are not just a person, but that your very nature is Divine.

As this experience expands and expands with daily, spiritual practice you realize that you have never been born and have never died – that you are *That* which is beyond the mind, body and senses – that you are *That* without beginning and without end – that you are eternal. This is the experience of immortality that Narada speaks of. Over time, with effective spiritual practice and true spiritual leadership in a Sadguru, you are able to operate from that place of the witness to your mind. You experience the indweller, the Self that observes all your thoughts and deeds.

In Nityananda Shaktipat Yoga, we refer to this as Witness Consciousness or spiritual witnessing awareness. As your spiritual witnessing awareness expands you are able to directly observe the play of the Shakti as this world and you come to know your place, your role, in that play. Over time and with spiritual practice and leadership, you come to realize that you are none of the roles you play, that the Self is the great actor and that you are *That*. This revelation of Grace frees you to Love.

Being *satisfied forever* is a matter of your becoming content with being content. This experience of contentment becomes your armor of Love. With content comes gratitude and gratitude gives rise to increased contentment. A grateful heart is a pure, loving heart that conquers all fear.

With contentment you become satisfied forever with knowing that you are awash in Love and gratitude. Contentment is freedom. However, being content does not mean that you become lazy. It does not mean that you don't engage in necessary activity to sustain your daily mundane existence. And it does not mean that you become complacent.

Here when I speak of contentment, this is a state in which you engage in all your activities with a one-pointed mind, with the intention of making your activities a blessed sacrament to God. This is a matter of perfecting your activity to glorify God. Blessed sacrament means that you engage in activity without wanting to possess the outcome, without wanting to possess people, places and things on some level. In this way, your daily activity becomes your offering to the Self, to God. This is how you become satisfied forever.

Again, many people are bartering and selling, in an exchange of limiting desire and craving. If all parties to the relating feel that the bartering and selling is equal, people call that Love. But that's not Love, that's infatuation.

That's infatuation that is driven by the limitation of the ego. Egoism is what causes us to want to manipulate and control outcomes. Most people who say that they're experiencing Love are actually infatuated with this process of bartering and selling in their attempt to manipulate and control outcomes.

Again, for Love to be Supreme, it has no attachments, no aversions, and it is unconditional. This unconditionality expands out of the effort to see God in everything and everyone, everywhere. Supreme Love begins with Love for God— and this is not Love for a God that is some far-off entity in the Heavens somewhere, or in a distant land. This is the understanding that God exists equally in each and every one of us, in everything, everywhere. When a person begins with this understanding, and begins to embrace this understanding, it becomes easier to gradually begin to express Love without conditions, even when boundaries are necessary.

Boundaries

I say 'even when boundaries are necessary' because often in relationships, friendships, intimate relationships, any kind of Love relationship or exchange of Love, there are issues with trust and respect. Often, people find that they have to have boundaries in order to command respect.

I'll give you an example: When I first took a Shaktipat Blessing Retreat with my Shri Gurudev many, many years ago, I had an incredible, exalted experience that lasted even after I left the retreat. During the retreat, I had placed some tilak on my forehead and when I returned home I didn't want to take it off. My friends who observed this thought I was crazy. They began to ask me, "Why are you wearing that?" and "Where have you been?" When I described where I had been and what I had experienced, they started to make fun of me.

This was the case also with family members, particularly with my father. He made a very bold move. He thought I needed an intervention and put together a family intervention with two psychotherapists and all the family members. I was invited to dinner with the family, and when I arrived, they hit me with this intervention. The psychotherapists began to ask me questions. My father stated all of his concerns and he said, "You've been brainwashed and you're in a cult." He talked about being frightened that I was going to be carted away on a bus to some farm somewhere. This was all a big game in his own mind, and he never asked me what I experienced. He never asked me what the ashram was like. He never asked me anything about my Guru.

So, I looked at my family members and the psychotherapists and said, "Have any of you been to my Guru's ashram? Have you experienced any of the programs? Have you met him? Have you had a chance to interact with him?" Of course, they all said, "No, why would we do that?" And then I said, "You all need to shut up. This is unintelligent behavior. What you should have done is you should have gone to several of my Gurudev's programs—you should have checked it out. You should have met him and had a chance to interact with him. That would have been the intelligent thing to do before attacking me as if I'm crazy. How would you know that it's a cult if you've never been there and had any experience for yourself? You've been watching television; you've been watching too many movies. You've been taking the advice of friends who have no idea because they've never been there." So, this is what I told them, and then I walked out.

My father contacted me after I walked out of the intervention and I said, "Look, I know how you feel about this, and you know how I feel about this. We can interact, we can share great times, we can spend time together, but my one term is that we do not discuss my Guru. Discussion of my Guru is off the table because I now know how you feel. We're not going to discuss it. We can discuss anything else." Well, he refused. He said, "I'm not abiding by that." And I said, "Well, fine. Then we're not going to have any interaction."

Five years went by. We had no discussion, no interaction. We did not speak to each other at all. And then, after five years, my stepmother (my second mom, as my father had remarried) called me and said, "We're having dinner. It's just going to be a handful of us. Would you like to come?" And I said, "Sure." When I arrived at dinner, my stepmom said, "Your father has something to tell you." And he said, "I went to your ashram. I stayed there for two weeks. I attended some programs. I thought it was very pleasant. I met your Guru." He was in the middle of writing a book, so he said, "I spent two weeks there, mostly locked in a room writing, but I did attend some programs, and I think, at least, it's better than drugs." Then he said, "I'm really happy for you."

For five years with that boundary, I never stopped loving my father. I loved him dearly, but the boundary that I established caused him to respect me and it forced him to actually do what I had told people in the intervention they should have done.

Even with boundaries, it is entirely possible to Love without conditions because, first and foremost, Love is an inner experience. The Siddhas of our Lineage say, "All the Love you give is really meant for you." When you give Love, you experience that Love for yourself; it's actually being directed at you when you give and express Love. Even in loving unconditionally, which is first and foremost an inner state, you can experience this Supreme Love, even when you have to draw boundaries.

This is not such a far-off experience. I'll give you another example. I've often asked mothers and fathers of children, "Have you ever had to really raise the bar? Your kids weren't listening to you, so you had to raise your voice; you had to yell at them, even though you didn't want to. Have you had the experience that, inside, you were really smiling, and you were kind of play-acting at yelling at them because it's not really what you wanted to do but you had to up the intensity?" They've all said yes. They all know that experience. This is just another example of being able to Love without conditions while expressing and acting on boundaries.

Love Yourself First

Love is only Love if it is first experienced inside *by loving yourself unconditionally*. This is where it starts. You can't Love others unconditionally if you don't Love yourself, even with all your foibles and mistakes, even with your notions that you might be impure or not able to measure up. Even with those notions, you have to start by loving yourself unconditionally, wherever you're at in this moment, at this time in your life. That has to happen first. You can't extend Supreme Love to others unless you have first extended it to yourself.

As you extend this unconditional Love to yourself, you begin to experience an expansion. Once you begin to Love yourself unconditionally, once you are engaged in the ability to laugh at yourself and love yourself, even regardless of your foibles, now you have the experience that then allows you to extend unconditional Love to others. But it can only be Love based on first seeing God in yourself, knowing that you are worthy of Self-Love because you are God, you are the Self, and then seeing God in everything and everyone else and also. This is how you avoid becoming infatuated.

Again, infatuation has to do with wanting to barter and trade needs for wants. And there are many people who have told me, and then I have observed their relationships, that they're in the relationship because they want to trade needs for wants, and they believe that's what relating is all about. If you're trading needs for wants and you feel that the trading is equal on the part of all parties to the relationship, that's infatuation.

Infatuation also occurs because in this trading of needs for wants, there is the desire to control outcomes. There is the desire to control people, places, and things on some level, to fulfill your own limiting desires and cravings. Again, a lot of people think that this is what Love is about, but that's not Love, that's infatuation. The infatuation increases if a person feels 'I'm getting everything I want, all of my limiting desires and cravings are being fulfilled.' This has absolutely nothing to do with Love.

I've seen many relationships over time break down because suddenly all parties to the relating do not feel that the bartering and trading is equal any longer. One person feels, 'Well, I'm giving you more than you're giving me' on that mundane level, and then the relationship starts to break down. Infatuation leaves the room and aversion sets in and then the relationship begins to deteriorate. But that's because it was never based on Supreme Love. Contrast that to people who you may know, and I certainly know, who are true friends. A true friend will extend Love to you regardless of what he or she is getting in return. A true friend will extend Love to you regardless of what you're into that the friend may not be interested in. A true friend will say, "Well, I'm not interested in that, but if it's what you want to do, I happily support you in it."

True friendship is a very good start in being able to interact with Supreme Love, being able to interact without conditions. I know many relationships that have prospered over a very long period of time, including marriages, because the people engaged in the relationship insisted on being each other's best friend, and that was the foundation for the relating. Those are the relationships that last and last and last.

The fact is the experience of Supreme Love makes you a better lover, a better friend, a better companion. This is what we have seen here in Nityananda Shaktipat Yoga.

Intimate Relating Without Love?

Can people be in an intimate relationship and not Love each other? Yes. And I've seen that a lot also. Again, there are all kinds of conditional relationships like this. Often, I've seen people agree: "You scratch my back, I'll scratch yours. Here are my terms, you tell me what your terms are and then we'll come to an agreement with the bartering and trading. Then if we agree on the bartering and trading, then we'll relate on that basis." This is where the phrase, "What's love got to do with it?" comes from—that famous song sung by Tina Turner.

"Are you giving me what I want, and are you getting what you want?" That's infatuation, and people who are infatuated don't necessarily love each other. For example, there are a lot of people who are engaged in relationships just because they want good sex. Everything else is secondary to the sex. Often, that is discussed before the relationship is entered into. So, that's the agreement. It has nothing to do with Love. "As long as the sex is great, we'll stay together. The minute it starts to decline, we're done." I'm just using this as one example.

Here's another example that is quite common; people who are stuck in a relationship where they are financially taken care of by someone else. They don't earn their own living. They enjoy this relationship where they get almost everything they want financially. They find themselves stuck because there is, of course, a trade-off to being kept financially, which is to endure, often, various types of abuse.

There are a lot of people who I know who enter into intimate relationships and marriages because of finances, because one or both parties want to agree on interacting based on money and the exchange of money. This is another common thing. That's also infatuation, which again, is enshrined in the limitation of the ego, this desire to manipulate and control outcomes to manipulate people, places and things on some level.

I know women and men who are in these kinds of relationships and they attempt to manipulate their lover based on sex. "You're not getting any until you write me a check for this," or "You're not getting any more until you buy me the jewelry I want, or until we take the vacation that I've been asking you for." These things are quite common. They have nothing to do with Love but there are people who make these agreements, either openly or subtly by way of surrendering to certain behaviors, and they just go along like that. Eventually, these relationships decline and they become difficult to remain in.

How Is Supreme Love Cultivated?

"A thousand half-loves must be forsaken to take one whole heart home."
~ Rumi, *Words of Paradise: Selected Poems of Rumi*

It is impossible to taste the sweet nectar of Love when the mind is restless. And when the mind remains restless, the heart is tainted with all kinds of impurities. So, to begin to cultivate Supreme Love, the restless mind must be arrested and made silent. *Happiness is a quiet mind.* Once the mind is trained to become quiet, the next step in cultivating Supreme Love is to purify the heart. There is so much talk of following your heart. In Nityananda Shaktipat Yoga we say that the heart has to be purified first, before it can be followed. Otherwise, there is confusion and more restlessness of the mind.

So, the first step is to purify the restless mind. The primary methods for doing so are the practice of True Meditation, the practice of Mantra Yoga, Chanting, Selfless Service and the study of the wisdom utterances of sages of steady wisdom. These steps, when taken together as part of a daily spiritual practice, begin to remove the dross that causes us to conceal our true nature from ourselves. Once we stop concealing our God nature from ourselves it becomes easy to summon the courage to Love, to dive into the ocean of Supreme Love.

True meditation is meditation on the Self. Over time, this brings the experience of the indescribable Joy of the Self that gradually leads to a quiet mind that is able to reflect Joy, Peace and Love. Meditating on the Self involves utilizing methods for increasing your spiritual witnessing awareness so that you are able to watch your thoughts passively, without any reaction our response. Then, these same methods carry you to that place that is beyond the mind and the senses.

The mind loves the places it frequents the most, you get what you meditate on and you become what you obey. If you engage effective methods for directing your mind inside to the Self, your mind will begin to love going there. With the right practice, Meditation on the Self brings the experience of indescribable Joy, over and over again. This is what you get when you meditate on the Self.

Therefore, if you meditate on pizza, money, sex or any limiting desire and craving you may have, that is what you are going to get, not the experience of the Bliss of the Self. Visualizing places in nature, beaches and oceans, flower gardens, etc. will only get you those with respect to your experience in meditation. There is nothing wrong with these, but meditating on them is not true Meditation. Meditating on those things will not get you the experience of the indescribable Joy of the Self. Instead, the restlessness of your mind will only increase while you attempt to meditate.

Mantra Yoga is both the understanding of the power of Mantra to purify the mind and the senses, as well as the practice of Mantra in doing so. Mantra is not just a name or reference to the Self. Mantra is God. This understanding is the basis for the practice of Mantra Yoga. In Nityananda Shaktipat Yoga we instruct people in the use of Chaitanya Mantras. Chaitanya Mantras are mantras that have been specifically given and practiced over millennia to quiet the restless mind and deliver you to that place beyond the mind and beyond the senses. These are powerful, spiritual Mantras that have proved effective over many centuries in making the restless mind quiet.

These Mantras are repeated inwardly and quietly at the start of Meditation. With practice and over time, they cause the restless mind to become silent and then dissolve. These Mantras are also repeated as one goes about his/her daily, mundane activities. This practice is known as Japa, Mantra repetition that is done mentally in the midst of activity. Chanting is another way in which these Mantras are used. The combination of Mantra repetition combined with the joy of song is a very powerful mechanism for making the restless mind quiet.

Why is it so important to quiet the restless mind? Because, when the mind is silent, Joy, the Bliss of the Self wells up automatically from inside. Then there is the experience of Supreme Love.

The Easy Means

The easy means to Meditation on the Self, your God nature, occurs by way of the full awakening of your spiritual witnessing awareness that lies dormant at the base of your spine in Muladhar chakra. This awakening happens by the transmission of the Grace-bestowing power of God known as *Shaktipat.* Authentic Shaktipat is offered by a Shaktipat Siddha Guru who is in a lineage of such Gurus. Lineage is essential because a Siddha Guru is authorized to give Shaktipat by his/her own Guru. This authorization includes that Guru, who is also a lineage holder, infusing his/her disciple with the full Shakti power to give Shaktipat.

I spent many years studying and practicing meditation with various teachers. I also lived in a Zen monastery for a while. In all that time, I never had even one experience of Bliss. In all that time, my mind never dissolved in meditation. Then I met my Guru and received Shaktipat from him. The difference in my meditations was immediate. Meditation became easier and more spontaneous. And, for the first time ever, I experienced silence of mind and my mind dissolving in Meditation. Great joy has been the result.

Here in Nityananda Shaktipat Yoga, there are a good number of experience shares offered by people who have received Shaktipat from Kedarji. You can see some of those shares in a video on the home page at NityanandaShakipatYoga.org. Shaktipat is an essential first step in taming the restless mind and purifying the heart.

After the receipt of Shaktipat, there are daily spiritual practices that are instructed by the Guru. These practices are time-honored and proved effective. When embraced and performed on a daily basis, over time, they make the restless mind quiet. They also sharpen the mind while also providing mental clarity. In order to cultivate Supreme Love, daily spiritual practice is necessary to wash away the dross that infects the mind and covers the heart. I have spoken about these practices in the previous section.

The Arc

The understandings we reach for dictate how we feel, along with the subsequent emotions connected to how we feel. That dictates how we are vibrating, what we project into Consciousness. And what we project into Consciousness always determines who and what we attract into our lives, including the situations and circumstances we find ourselves in. So, if we want to change how we are vibrating and how we feel, we have to change the understandings that we reach for and embrace. In Nityananda Shaktipat Yoga we call this the principle of The Arc. Then there is the practice of The Arc. The practice of The Arc begins with an examination of the understandings we embrace.

An examination of these understandings is essential for experiencing what Love is, and for cultivating that Love. This examination begins with reviewing the understandings you currently hold about Love, along with an examination of where you got those understandings from.

Where have you gotten your understandings from about love?

The Story of the Kalpavriksha Tree

There was a man whose karmas were such that he always seemed to meet with poor circumstances. At one point he felt that he could do nothing right and began to give up any hope of living. One day he decided to leave his house and just walk in no particular direction. He thought he would just walk and walk and walk until he dropped dead. After he had walked for a while, he began to hear footsteps behind him. So, he walked faster. As he sped up the footsteps sped up. When he slowed down, the footsteps slowed down. Finally, he quickly turned around to see who was following him. It was a stranger with a curious smile.

The stranger said, "I know your predicament. If you follow me, I can take you to a place where you can solve your problems." The man agreed to follow the stranger. He was taken a good distance to a clearing in a field. On the other side of that clearing was a very tall tree. The stranger said, "Sit under this tree. It is the wish-fulfilling tree. Whatever you want just think of it and that is what will manifest for you." The man looked at the tree and formulated a question. But when he turned to ask his question the stranger was gone.

So, the man sat under the tree and immediately felt very relaxed. He then began to think, "I want a beautiful mansion to live in with many rooms." The moment he thought this, a mansion appeared in front of him. This place was huge. He got up and walked around in it. There were many beautiful rooms. There were big gardens with flowers, bushes and groves of small trees. He thought to himself, "Who will care for this place? I need servants and gardeners." The moment he had this thought, the servants appeared. He began to tell them to clean the place and care for the gardens and tree groves. Then he sat back under the tree, staring at this place.

Then he had another thought. "This place is so large. I'm not going to live in it all by myself. I need a woman to share this mansion with and she has to be young, sexy, and voluptuous." The moment he had this thought, the woman appeared before him. And she had everything in all the right places. "Wow," he thought. He sat the woman down next to him under that tree.

After staring into each other's eyes for a while the man thought, "I want chefs to cook meals for us. I want a five-course meal right now." Immediately the chefs appeared and he instructed them in what to cook. The five-course meal was prepared and the chefs brought out each course, one at a time. The man and the woman sat under the tree and began to feed each other the food.

As they were enjoying the meal, the man looked around at all that had manifested, and then looked at the woman. Then he thought,

"Wait a minute. This can't be real. How could all this be happening to me? It must be some kind of trick. I've been duped! This must be the work of some demon." At that moment, a demon appeared with long, sharp teeth and big jaws. He ate the man in one bite and spit out his bones.

Well, would it be so that you could manifest in form all that you want at a mere thought and snap of a finger. However, the story is an illustration of the principle of The Arc.

In Nityananda Shaktipat Yoga, we offer a contemplation that helps people to practice The Arc, beginning with an examination. Up until the moment you began reading this book, where have you gotten your understandings from about love? Note as many of the following that apply to you.

- Your parents.
- Close friends.
- Other family members.
- Authority figures in your life growing up.
- Books (ex: romance novels).
- Television.
- Movies.
- The Internet.
- Popular culture.
- Accepted fantasies that you have gotten from others.
- Early role models.
- Mentors in your life.
- An infatuation and belief in the 'soul mate' theory.

The Practice of The Arc

After reviewing the above list, it is likely that you will also come to the conclusion that you have never really questioned or fully examined the understandings you embrace regarding love. Have you simply accepted these understandings as they were presented to you, because they are popular and accepted by others?

The practice of The Arc is simple. For the sake of this example, let's assume that you want to experience Supreme Love that is not dependent on anything or anyone outside yourself – that you want to love unconditionally and with a pure heart. This, of course, requires courage – the courage to Love.

The first step is to reevaluate your understandings about what love is, based on where those understandings came from. My Guru created a vast, worldwide community of spiritual beings who wanted the experience of what Love really is. He, himself, was a Self-realized Love being who offered so much Love and Compassion to the world. Keeping his company allowed me to closely observe that Supreme Love is not just for saints. In his company I experienced that this Love is an innate quality in all of us that we conceal from ourselves.

My Guru taught the practice of The Arc as a means for so many of us to understand and experience what Love is. As I reevaluated the understandings about love that I had reached for and embraced before meeting my Guru, I realized that I had accepted a notion of love that made it impossible for me to experience that which makes Love Supreme. Every item on the above list applied to me. I had fashioned a notion about love by accepting other people's notions and ideas about love. And these other people did not have an experience of what makes love Supreme, and I wanted that experience.

The following is an excerpt taken from *The Essential Rumi* translated by Coleman Banks.

GREEN EARS

There was a long drought. Crops dried up. The vineyard leaves turned black.

People were gasping and dying like fish thrown up on the shore and left there. But one man was always laughing and smiling.

A group came and asked, "Have you no compassion for this suffering?" The man answered, "To your eyes this is a drought. To me, it is a form of God's joy."

Everywhere in this desert I see green corn growing waist high, a sea-wilderness of young ears greener than leeks. I reach to touch them. How could I not?

When you make peace with your father (God), he will look peaceful and friendly. The whole world is a form for truth.

When someone does not feel grateful to That, the forms appear *as he feels*. They mirror his anger, his greed, and his fear. Make peace with the universe. Take joy in it.

It will turn to gold. Resurrection will be now.
Every moment, a new beauty. And never any
boredom! Instead, this abundant, pouring noise
of many springs in your ears.

The tree limbs will move like people dancing,
who suddenly know what the mystical life is. The
leaves snap their fingers like they're hearing
music. They are! A sliver of a mirror shines out
from under a felt covering. Think how it will be
when the whole thing is open to the air and the
sunlight!
~ *Mevlana Rumi*

By making peace with God you set the
stage to experience the indescribable Joy of the
true Heart, the Self. *That Joy is Love.* It is
Supreme. Once you taste the nectar of that Bliss,
there is nothing else you want more. And this is
the foundation for taking up the highest
understandings of what Love is, along with the
practices mentioned above for cultivating
Supreme Love. The understandings you reach for
and embrace are everything.

So, reach for the highest. Let the wisdom
of the Self-realized Love Beings lead you. By
imbibing that wisdom and engaging the practices
I discussed earlier in this chapter, you will begin
to taste the elixir of Love. Then, as you apply that
experience to your daily mundane existence, you
will come to fully understand what makes Love
Supreme and why it is the greatest power in the
universe.

What Is Courage?

Courage is the absence of fear, embodied in Supreme Love. This combination equals fearlessness. Fear and Love cannot co-exist. Where there is one there is the absence of the other. Therefore, courage is required to Love and, with Love, you become fearless.

My Guru offered three world tours in which he travelled the globe offering programs. During one of those tours, when he was in California, I was assigned to his security detail. At the end of the evening programs, Baba offered Darshan which is a time when people can come forward to be greeted by the Guru and blessed. There were thousands of people attending these programs. For Darshan, people formed several lines to move in an orderly fashion down the center of the hall to where Gurudev sat in his chair.

The Shakti power of such beings brings out both the best and the worst in people. During his world tours, there had been several incidents of people attempting some kind of attack on Baba. So, security in the hall had been stepped up. My post was to stand behind Baba's chair when Darshan started. There were several other security personnel posted at various points around the Darshan line.

One evening during Darshan, a man came down the Darshan line and, as I observed how he was dressed and the position of his hands, it appeared to me that he was carrying a weapon, hidden under his jacket. I signaled to two other people on the security detail who then joined the line behind this person. When the man got to Baba's chair, he stood over Baba, staring at him. Then he drew a gun and pointed it at Baba's face. The man blurted out something unintelligible while doing so.

Baba looked at the man with so much Love. Then Gurudev told him, "I am ready to go to God in this moment. But you are not ready. You still have not made peace with God and have so many karmas to face. So, you should think twice before you pull that trigger. And if you decide to shoot me now, just know that I love you."

The man was in a state of shock. He blurted out, "You're crazy!" At that moment, the three of us who had now surrounded this person jumped him, disarmed him and started beating on him. After that, it was our intention to hold him for the police. As we were beating the man, Baba yelled, "Stop. What are you doing!?" Gurudev then told us to let the man go, saying that he would never return. So, we let him go and he never did return. This event stuck with me for a very long time.

Several years later, I was in Manhattan, on my way to Gurudev's Manhattan ashram to attend an evening program. As I walked to the ashram I heard screaming from behind me. I turned to find an elderly couple. The husband was lying on the ground with his wife crouched over him. I started to help the man up. Then he told me that a mugger had stolen his briefcase with something very valuable inside. The man begged me to retrieve the briefcase. I don't know what got in me in that moment, but I began chasing the mugger who I could still see at a distance down the block. What was I thinking!?

I ran as fast as I could. As I began to catch up with the mugger, I heard someone behind me. Then I felt the barrel of a gun on the back of my head. As it turned out, there were two perpetrators. The man holding a gun to my head said, "Don't try to be a hero. Otherwise, you'll die tonight." I spun around and starred the gunman in the eye. At that moment, the words of my Guru from that incident when he was assaulted in the program hall in California flooded my mind. With the gun now pointed at my forehead I said, "I am ready to go to God in this moment. But you, my friend, are not. You have not made peace with your maker. Just know that if you decide to shoot me now, I love you." The gunman quickly removed the gun from my head and ran away.

Kali Yuga

The current age is what is known in our Yoga as the Kali Yuga Age. It is the last in a world cycle of four ages. These world cycles have been coming and going since the beginning of time. Each age has specific qualities and ramifications. There are debilitating qualities of this Kali Yuga age that, when understood, will help you to imbibe the spiritual urgency of our times and the necessity for the courage to love. Some of those qualities are:

• A time ruled by lust, wanton sex, the pursuit of personal power and collective greed.
• Dominated by people's attachment to words, causing the brainwashing of the masses and mind control where attachment to pleasure and pain are concerned.

• The destruction of true spiritual awareness in favor of false notions like God is the body and what can be acquired and enjoyed through the senses.
• Abandonment of the common good and abandonment of Liberty in favor of government control of people's minds and speech.
• The complete decline of the collective spiritual awareness of the masses.
• Taking refuge in the personal gain of people, places and things.
• The pursuit of monetary wealth and fame and the worship of these.
• A pill for everything, expressed as the desire of the masses to take refuge in mind-altering drugs that cause the increased desire for fantasy fulfillment.
• The increased preference for superficiality by the masses.
• The decline of Human Dignity, especially where female-embodied beings are concerned.

To rise above these debilitating qualities in order to experience the freedom of Supreme Love *requires courage*. Courage is innate in you. Your courage is summoned by the recognition of God in everything and everyone, everywhere. This recognition gradually becomes constant through the performance of spiritual practices - those practices that I shared in the last chapter.

Why Is Fearlessness Important?

As I stated earlier, Fear and Love cannot co-exist. Where there is one there is the absence of the other. This is why the attainment of fearlessness is so important.

In the Bhagavad Gita, Lord Krishna states that, of all these divine qualities, fearlessness holds the highest place. Listen to what it is. And, in his commentary on this verse contained in the sacred text *Jnaneshwari*, Shri Jnaneshwar states:

"One who does not leap into a flood can have no fear of being drowned, nor can one who lives a temperate life be in dread of illness. So the person who does not allow egotism to arise in connection with good and evil deeds and abandons the anxieties of worldly life, and through the realization of non-duality knows all others to be one with himself, casts out all fear."

In the Upanishads it states: "dviteeyaadvai bhayam bhavati" - "One who perceives that there are others will be in fear." The root cause of all fear is your notion that you are separate from God; a notion that you yourself create by your power of concealment. You conceal your true nature, that you are one with the Self; you conceal this fact from yourself. This is the root cause of all your fears.

Fear is an energy that we create for ourselves and then run from, like the guy who saw his shadow and thought it was a demon coming to get him. In fact, fear is the shadow of truth. We are told that fear is a natural state - that it is natural for us to fear, that this is a standard part of the human condition for all people. But this is not true. In fact, we create our fears.

Entanglement in comfort, security and reward causes many diverse fears to manifest, from the most insignificant to the most traumatic. Over many, many lifetimes these fears are embedded in your memory and manifest as your Karmas. They culminate in your clinging to life out of fear of loss and death. To eliminate all fears one has to take total refuge in God. And to accomplish this requires spiritual practice under the leadership of a Sadguru.

These are some of the ways in which people conceal their God nature from themselves, making it impossible to experience Supreme Love. Note how many apply to you.

- You make yourself small to fit in or to be accepted by others because you don't want to be rejected or abandoned.

- You forget who you really are. This is due to a lack of spiritual awareness and direct experience of the Self.

- Your spiritual, witnessing awareness is not expanded and, therefore, you think you are over something challenging, unpleasant or traumatic when you are not.

- You forget that you are responsible for the play of your existence here – that you create the karmas that then bind you.

- You believe yourself to be small, a sinner, a doer who must make things happen.

- You keep useless inner and outer company. This act of concealment is a major barrier to the experience of what Love is.

This reminds me of a story. A king and his son, the prince, went hunting in a forest riding the same horse. The king wanted to hunt deer and found one deep in the forest. But whenever the king drew his bow and arrow to shoot the deer, the deer disappeared. In this way, the deer kept eluding the king. Dusk came and the king was very upset that he had not bagged the deer. He decided he would follow the deer's tracks deep into the forest, in an attempt to kill the deer before nightfall.

The king told his son, the prince to dismount. He told the prince that it would be easier and safer if he went the rest of the way alone because it was getting dark. The king told the prince to sit under a tree, and that he would be back for the prince once he had bagged the deer.

The prince sat under the tree, waiting for his father to return. Night came and went but there was no sign of the king. Then, late in the morning, some hunters were on foot in the forest and came across the prince. They asked why he was sitting there under that tree and how long he had been there. The boy explained the situation without telling the hunters that he was the crown prince and his father was the king, as he did not trust them not to be hostile toward the crown. He told the hunters that he was hungry and thirsty. He also said that he was concerned that his father had gotten lost in the forest. The hunters lived in a small village on the other side of the forest. So, they took the boy with them and returned to their village.

Another day passed and then the king made his way back through the forest, not having found the deer. The king went to the area where he thought he left the prince sitting under the tree. Not having found the prince there, the king became frantic and began searching the forest, to no avail. The king then returned to the palace and gathered his ministers and an army battalion. This search party fanned out through the forest searching for the boy.

Five days passed and, finally, the prime minister told the king that it was likely that the boy had been carried away by wild animals and eaten. The search was called off and a funeral ceremony was offered for the death of the boy.

Several years passed. Then, one day, the prime minister was sent to all of the villages in the kingdom to find able-bodied young men to draft into the king's army. The prime minister arrived at the hunter's village. These people lived in poverty and wore burlap sacs for clothing. They rarely bathed so they stunk.

The prime minister demanded that all of the young men line up in the village square. He then began inspecting the men, one by one. As he went down the line, he came to the prince. The boy was dressed like all the others and had long hair and a beard. The prime minister looked carefully at the boy and then exclaimed, "You are the crown prince! We thought you were dead. Come. We must return you to the palace and your king." The young man replied, "No. I am no such person. I'm just an ordinary hunter like the rest." Due to keeping the company of the hunters, the prince had come to believe that he was one of them. He had come to think and act like them and had concealed his royalty from himself.

This what happens when you don't keep the best, the most useful inner and outer company. You begin to think that you are just small, just ordinary or delightfully weird. And this prevents you from drowning in the ocean of Love.

How Is Fearlessness Cultivated?

"The abstinent run away from what they desire but carry their desires with them. When a person merges with this Love, that person leaves all desires behind."
~ *Shri Krishna, from the Bhagavad Gita*

For love to be love it cannot be dependent on anything or anyone outside yourself. To experience the supremacy of Love it is essential that you address your limiting desires and cravings for people, places and things. What makes a desire or craving limited is the desire to manipulate or control the outcome, the result of your desiring. Wanting to control outcomes conceals the experience of Supreme Love because, with the desire to possess outcomes, egoism expands. Fear is an ego expression and a natural progression of the desire to possess outcomes. And where there is fear, there cannot be the experience of Love.

The key to loving in a way that frees you is not to abstain from activity and interaction with others, but to interact without wanting to possess outcomes. Love is freeing, not binding. The experience of Love frees you in every way, in the absence of fear.

If you don't know who you are, you will become whoever and whatever others want you to be. So, the first step to cultivating fearlessness is to know, to have the direct experience of who you are, and to expand that experience.

Once there was a mighty king named Janaka. One evening King Janaka had a vivid dream that frightened him. He dreamt that he was a beggar who had gone without food for 15 days. As this beggar, he finally found a shelter, but it was closing just as he arrived. Standing at the gate of this shelter, he begged for food. He was told that all of the food had already been given away for the day. The King begged that the bowl from which the food had been distributed be scraped, and the scraps given to him.

One of the attendants grudgingly did this and gave him a little bit of spiced vegetable in his tin plate. He staggered across the road into a field and sat down to eat the tiny portion. In that same field there were two bulls fighting. Upon seeing him, one of the bulls charged him and tossed the food up into the air, scattering it everywhere.

Just at that moment, finding himself in a state of horror, his eyes opened to find that he was, in fact, King Janaka lying in his royal bed, being fanned by his queens. Closing his eyes, again he found himself to be the beggar sitting in the field, confronted by the bull. When he opened his eyes again, he was the King.

Janaka became obsessed. Who was he? The King or the beggar? Was the identity of one more real than the other? So, the King issued a proclamation that all the sages and sadhus in the kingdom should be summoned to his court to interpret his dream. They were all brought to the palace. When none of them could interpret his dream, Janaka had them all imprisoned.

One of the imprisoned sages had a son who was deformed in 8 places. The son's name was Ashtavakra which means deformed in 8 places. Ashtavakra was a great Siddha who was known in the kingdom as the boy sage. When he heard that his father was in prison on the order of the King, he immediately went to the palace and demanded to see the King.

When Ashtavakra entered the King's court, upon seeing his deformities and the jerking way in which he moved, everyone in the court began laughing a him. To their astonishment, Ashtavakra himself began to laugh out loud, whereupon a sudden hush came over the entire court.

"Who are you boy? And what are you laughing at? asked Janaka. Ashtavakra replied, "I have heard such great things about you King Janaka, and the splendor of your court. But I now see that you are just a pack of leather merchants. You look at me and you only see the external skin and the deformity of my body. You are blind to that spirit that animates it. Now ask your question so that my father can go free."

Astonished at Ashtavakra's authority and spiritual radiance, the King explained his dream. "Oh King, when you are a beggar in your dream, being a King is not a reality for you. And, when you are a King, being a beggar is also not a reality. In fact, neither identity is real. Reality is that from which both identities are projected – the pure, the Absolute witness, the Self." King Janaka's confusion vanished. His mind was enlightened and he became the disciple of Ashtavakra.

Steps to Cultivating Fearlessness

Remember that Love and fear cannot co-exist. Where there is one there is the absence of the other. All notions, all ideas and thoughts, all the forms, all manner of expressions – all of these emanate from the Self. The Self is the creator and possessor of all these things. Therefore, the Self fears nothing and no one. And you are that Self, the One God that exists inside you as you.

So, the first step in cultivating fearlessness is to have and then expand your direct experience of the Self, God. This is accomplished by way of the daily spiritual practices that I spoke of in Chapter 1. I will list them again here:

- Meditation
- The practice of Mantra Yoga
- Chanting
- Selfless Service
- The Study of the Wisdom Utterances of Sages of Steady Wisdom

As stated in Chapter 1, the mind loves the places it frequents the most, you get what you meditate on and you become what you obey. If you engage effective methods for directing your mind inside to the Self, your mind will begin to love going there. With the right practice, Meditation on the Self brings the experience of indescribable Joy, over and over again. This is what you get when you meditate on the Self.

So, to cultivate fear, we begin by working with the mind to make the restless mind quiet. Calming the restless mind is essential. Happiness is a quiet mind. From that happiness springs peace and the experience of the indescribable Joy of the Self. Fearlessness rises out of this Joy.

The mind can be made silent to the point where you are able to only engage your mind when it is necessary to perform tasks. This is similar to turning a computer off when you are done using it. Meditation on the Self is vital in this process of making the mind silent. There are two experiences to attain in this regard. The first and the easier of the two is known as Savikalpa Samadhi. This is the experience of the Bliss of the Self when there are still some thoughts in the mind. The second that comes with extended practice is Nirvikalpa Samadhi. This is the experience of the mind becoming silent and then dissolving when meditating. The goal of perfecting Savikalpa Samadhi is to begin to experience Nirvikalpa Samadhi.

"You are the one witness of everything and are always completely free. The cause of your bondage is that you see the witness as something other than this."
~ *Ashtavakra, from his Ashtavakra Gita*

We know when we are thinking but how do we know we are thinking? How do we know we have slept? How do we know we have dreamt? We know because there is a higher power, a power that we refer to as the Knower, the Witness, that Supreme Principle that is beyond the mind and beyond the senses. That is what observes these changing states of experience. That Witness is who we really are.

Witness Consciousness, also known as the state of the Observer, is an experience in which you are able to watch your thoughts, emotions, notions, etc. come and go passively, without judgment and without any reaction or response that allows the energy of egoism to arise. This is an experience in which, from that Witness to your mind, you are able to observe that Source from which all thoughts rise, are sustained and

withdrawn. This is the state of Savikalpa
Samadhi. This is where to begin.

In Nityananda Shaktipat Yoga, we offer a
practice known as Witness Consciousness
Centering. This practice utilizes specific forms of
contemplation to expand the experience of the
Witness to your mind. Go to this web page for
instruction to begin practicing Witness
Consciousness Centering:
https://nityanandashaktipatyoga.org/dharanas.
html
There is also a book on this practice entitled *The
Verses On Witness Consciousness* that you can
purchase here:
https://www.nityanandashaktipatyoga.org/the-
verses-on-witness-consciousness/

As your experience of Savikalpa Samadhi
grows, you will naturally want more of the
experience of a quiet and silent mind. This
experience comes with engaging in the practices
I have mentioned above, under the leadership of
a Sadguru. The receipt of Shaktipat is the best
foundation for your experience and expansion of
these practices. You can learn more about
Shaktipat here:
https://www.shaktipatblessing.org/about-
shaktipat/

Engaging in the methods and practices
discussed above, your mind will gradually
become quieter and quieter. In turn, this will
give rise to more and more of the experience of
the indescribable Joy of the Self that is your God
nature. And, with that growing experience,
fearlessness will grow within you. It all starts
with your addressing what's in your mind by
first observing all the places you allow your mind
to wander to. This will enable you to begin
reigning in your restless mind by training it to

turn within to the Self. To begin to experience fearlessness, *a quality that is innate within you*, it is essential that you quiet your mind and keep your mind quiet.

Grace Is The Ocean of Love

Grace is the power, the Love that rescues us from the entanglement of worldliness and, like a boat, carries us across the illusion of this world to that distant shore of Joy, Peace and the Bliss of the Absolute. Grace is that which frees us from the bondage of ignorance that keeps God concealed from us. Grace is the gift of life. In this regard, my Guru used to say, "Therefore, you should realize your true worth and set your daily routine accordingly."

Grace is God's gift to us. God is the Guru-principle that becomes the living Siddha Guru in order to transmit God's Grace to seekers of the Truth who want to drown in the ocean of Supreme Love to gain their freedom. The living Shaktipat Siddha Guru bestows Shaktipat, the Grace-bestowing power of God, in order to enact the rescue of living beings. This rescue begins the journey to Love. What are the obstacles to this journey? In this regard, my Guru used to tell a story.

"For the sake of joy, a person does all kinds of things, not knowing that happiness lies within. Such a person is like the musk deer that carries the precious fragrance of musk in its own navel. But out of ignorance, the musk deer keeps searching for that fragrance outside. The breeze carries the fragrance of the musk toward the mountains, and the deer runs eagerly in that direction.

It runs and runs searching for that fragrance and eventually it dies. Then the people who live in the mountains cut open the deer and remove the musk. It is the same story with a human being. In spite of everything one does, a person does not see lasting happiness. But if, by good fortune, he meets a saint, a great being, then a person can become completely happy."

You are the Love you seek. And all the Love you give is really meant for you. So, why do you go looking for love when you are that love? This is why I have shared the story of the musk deer. To experience that you are Love, to experience that Love exists right inside you requires Grace. And coming to dwell in the endless ocean of Love means coming to live in a state of Grace. That state is freedom. Experiencing and understanding the workings of Grace does require that you become established in a daily spiritual practice that gives you contact with that Love, the Self, on a daily basis.

So many people complain that they can't find love or are unlucky in love. That's because they are looking for it where it is not - like looking for water in a desert when you actually live by the ocean. To find, experience and drown in Love, you have to look for it where it is, inside you.

Another obstacle to this is the inner and outer company you keep. My Guru used to say, "Just a drop of sour curd can spoil an entire ocean of milk. So too useless company can lead to every kind of evil. It can make you gossip about others and speak ill of them; It can make you indiscreet, arrogant, impure, full of animosity; useless company can make you behave dishonestly. Therefore, students of our

Siddha Science must be extremely careful to avoid useless company and to keep the best inner and outer company."

The Story of Kaikeyee and Mantharaa

King Dasharatha had two wives who were his Queens – Kaikeyee and Kausalyaa. Kausalyaa was the mother of Rama and Kaikeyee was the mother of Bharata. The two Queens were full of love for the kingdom and the royal family. They were filled with affection for one another and lived embracing modesty.

Kaikeyee had a maid-servant named Mantharaa. The two had grown up together in a small village, before Kaikeyee married the King. When she did, it was Mantharaa's great fortune to be taken in as Kaikeyee's maid-servant, as this took her out of the poverty she had lived in for most of her life growing up. These two had become close friends and Mantharaa was Kaikeyee's confidant. The two spent all of their days together shopping in the markets and enjoying the palace gardens and horseback riding.

The day came when King Dasharatha had to place a successor on the throne. He chose Rama over Bharata, as Rama was loved by the entire kingdom and, having become the disciple of the Siddha Guru Vashistha, had become very wise. He was also a formidable warrior. The people in the kingdom rejoiced at Rama being chosen as the new King. There were celebrations day and night, and people danced in the streets.

All of this angered Mantharaa. She approached Kaikeyee and said that, if Rama were to sit on the throne, she and Kaikeyee and Bharata would lose their royal status and become ordinary servants in the palace. She said that Kausalyaa, Rama's mother, would be favored over Kaikeyee. Mantharaa convinced Kaikeyee the only way to prevent this was for her to convince her husband the King that her own son, Bharata, should sit on the throne and that Rama should be removed as heir. Knowing that Rama's brother Lakshmana, who also commanded the armies of the King would likely execute a coup against the King to ensure that Rama is placed on the throne, Mantharaa told Kaikeyee that Rama and his wife Seetaa would have to be banished from the kingdom to be certain that Bharata would remain King.

Mantharaa reminded Kaikeyee that King Dasharatha owed her a boon for her having saved his life on the battlefield by dragging him to safety when he was wounded. At that time, the King had told Kaikeyee that he would grant her any boon she asked for and she told the King that she would wait until some future date to request the boon. And so, having convinced Kaikeyee of what must be done, the plan was hatched. Kaikeyee approached her husband the King and reminded him of the boon he promised. The King told her to ask and she did.

Kaikeyee told him that he must remove Rama as heir to the throne to make her own son, Bharata the new King. Then she explained to the King that, in order to secure Bharata's reign, there mustn't be any opposition from Lakshmana who controlled the armed forces. To ensure that didn't happen, the King must strip Rama and Seetaa of all their possessions and banish them from the kingdom for 14 years. Upon hearing this request, the King begged

Kaikeyee to ask him for anything else but that. Then he fainted.

When the King came to he told his wife that he was a man of his word and sent one of his guards to fetch Rama. Rama was found in the fields with his brother Lakshmana. They were summoned to the King and rushed to court. When they arrived, they found all the King's ministers present, along with Kaikeyee, Mantharaa and Kausalyaa. King Dasharatha announced that he had changed his mind, and that Bharata would be coronated as the new King. He also announced that Rama and Seetaa had 24 hours to give away all their possessions, and that they were banished to the forest on the outskirts of the kingdom for 14 years.

Immediately understanding what happened, Lakshmana railed against Kaikeyee. He accused the King of not being fit to make such a decision and implored Rama to give him the word so that he could command the armies to imprison the King, Kaikeyee and Mantharaa to ensure Rama's place on the throne. Rama had a very pure mind that was steeped in gratitude and surrender. He understood everything taking place to be the will of God and a matter of God's Grace.

Rama agreed to his father's terms. Lakshmana then told Rama, "I'm coming with you. I will not stay here without your rule." Rama looked at Kaikeyee with compassion. He then told Lakshmana to stay behind to guard Kaikeyee, as he expected that there might be attempts on her life when the public found out what had just happened. Rama and Seetaa then gave away all their possessions and left the palace to dwell in the forest for 14 years. Bharata refused to sit on the throne, placing Rama's sandals on the seat instead. Bharata then agreed to manage the daily affairs of the kingdom in Rama's name, until Rama's return.

The kingdom had been terrorized on a constant basis by the demon King Raavana. The outcome of this story is that, while exiled in the forest, Raavana kidnapped Seetaa. This act set up a confrontation between Rama and Raavana that led to a war in which the demon King and his forces were destroyed, thus freeing the kingdom from terror. Rama and Seetaa were than welcomed back to the kingdom and Rama took his rightful place on the throne.

This story illustrates what can happen when one does not keep the best inner and outer company, and also what happens when one keeps the company of the Self. Over time, the Grace inherent in direct contact with and experience of the Self, yields the experience of Supreme Love everywhere and in all matters.

By God's Grace

Love is an ocean of Grace that transforms you from the inside out. By God's Grace the Ocean of Love is attained. In the *Narada Bhakti Sutras*, also known as *Narada's Way of Divine Love*, Shri Narada states the following:

"When all thoughts, all words, and all deeds are given up to the Lord, and when the least forgetfulness of God makes one intensely miserable, then Love has begun."

In Nityananda Shaktipat Yoga we focus on engaging in activity and performing tasks to experience the indescribable Joy of the Self. To accomplish this requires performing deeds without the desire to manipulate, control or possess outcomes in any way. This means making every task, every deed a blessed sacrament, an offering to God. In this offering there is great Bliss. The indescribable Joy of the Self causes one to remember God. Having tasted the nectar of Self-awareness in this way, as the experience of Joy expands the absence of it makes one intensely miserable.

It is through this experience and the expansion of it that you come to know that Grace is the Ocean of Love. Joy is the fuel for this experience of Supreme Love. Joy brings the true understanding of what happiness is. From that experience you become free. The necessity to experience Joy in daily living can never be overemphasized. It is only out of Joy that Love can be experienced and understood as being Supreme.

God Loves a Grateful Heart

God loves grateful heart. You can only know what Love is through gratitude because gratitude purifies the heart. Gratitude is not only the greatest of virtues, but the parent of all the others. A great being has said, "Blessed are those who can give without remembering and receive without forgetting." And here in Nityananda Shaktipat Yoga we have a saying: Thank you Lord for another day to glorify you.

A grateful heart is a pure heart that is then able to drown in the ecstasy of Love. Gratitude begins with cultivating humility – a state of Grace borne of Equality Consciousness and steeped in awe. This is a state that requires the complete recognition of Grace at all times, in all situations and circumstances.

The recognition of Grace is the highest understanding of the Play of the Shakti as this world where Chit Shakti is the possessor of all people, places and things. Becoming humble in this way manifests reverence – reverence for the Guru and God – That One that is reflected in all people, places and things. This reverence completes the experience of awe contained in humility by cultivating Bhakti – your Devotion and Longing to be free.

The result of your experience of Bhakti is that you become content, and this experience of contentment gives rise to more and more gratitude. Once the heart is purified in this way it becomes easy to see God in everything and everyone, everywhere. This leads to a state of indescribable Joy that persists and persists and persists. In this experience there is the recognition that the ocean of Love is a treasure of Grace.

The Story of Ron Cotton

It was hot and humid in Burlington, N.C. on the night of July 28, 1984. Jennifer Thompson, then a 22-year-old college student, had gone to bed early in her off-campus apartment. As she slept, a man shattered the light bulb near her back door, cut her phone line, and broke in.

"I remember kind of waking up and turning my head to the side and saying, 'Who's there? Who is it?' And I saw the top of someone's head kind of sliding beside my mattress. I screamed and I felt a blade go to my throat," Thompson told 60 Minutes correspondent Lesley Stahl.

Thompson said the man, armed with a knife, told her to shut up or that he would kill her. Her first thought was to offer him anything she had to go away. "You can have my credit card. You can have my wallet. You can have anything in the apartment. You can have my car." And he looked at me and said, "I don't want your money." "And I knew what was getting ready to happen."

She vowed to stay alert and study him so that if she lived, she could help put him away forever. After about half an hour, Thompson tricked the rapist into letting her get up and fix him a drink; she ran out the back door. He fled and raped a second woman half a mile away. Detective Mike Gauldin met Thompson at the hospital. "The first comment I remember her making was, 'I'm gonna get this guy that did this to me.' She said, 'I took the time to look at him. I will be able to identify him if I'm given an opportunity,'" Gauldin remembered. Asked if she had been able to pick out any distinguishing characteristics, Thompson told Stahl, "He had a pencil-thin mustache. His eyes were almond shaped."

Detective Gauldin worked with Thompson to make a composite sketch, poring over eyes, noses, ears and lips in an effort to try to recreate the face she had seen that night. The sketch went out, and tips started coming in. One of those tips was about a young man named Ronald Cotton. He worked at a restaurant near the scene of both rapes and had a record: a guilty plea to breaking and entering, and as a teenager, to sexual assault. Three days after the rape, Gauldin called Thompson in to do a photo lineup. He laid six pictures down on the table, said the perpetrator may or may not be one of them, and told her to take her time.

Gauldin said Thompson did not immediately identify a photo, taking her time to study each picture. According to the police report, Thompson studied the pictures for five minutes. "She picked up Ron Cotton's photograph and said, 'That's the man who raped me,'" Gauldin recalled. He said Thompson was sure she had identified the right man.

Cotton heard the news from his mother's boyfriend. "He comes in and gives me a very detailed account of where he was, who he was with that night. As it turns out, that was a false alibi," Gauldin said. "I realized later that I had got my weekends confused, so therefore it gave them reason to think that I was lying," Cotton explained. Cotton went to the police to clear his name, but he didn't get to leave. He was locked up, and days later put in a physical lineup. Gauldin says the men in the lineup were asked to step forward, speak, and step back. And then Thompson identified number five, Ronald Cotton. She told the detectives that she was absolutely sure it was him.

In a week-long trial, the jury heard about Cotton's faulty alibi, his clothing that matched Thompson's description, and a piece of foam found on her floor that seemed to come from one of his shoes. And most powerfully, they heard from Thompson. In court, when asked if she recognized her rapist, she named Ronald Cotton.

It took the jury just 40 minutes to reach a verdict: guilty on all counts. Ron Cotton was sentenced to life plus 50 years. This meant he would die in prison. Ronald Cotton was handcuffed, shackled, and taken to North Carolina's Central Prison. He was 22 years old.

He started working in the prison kitchen, singing in the choir, and writing letter after letter to his attorneys, hoping to get a new trial. Then one day as he watched a new inmate being brought in, he had a strange feeling. "I said, 'Excuse me.' I said, 'You look familiar.' I said, 'Where are you from?'" He said, 'I'm from Burlington.' 'I said, 'I am too.' I said, 'You kind of resembling the drawing of a suspect in a crime in which I'm falsely imprisoned for. Did you commit this crime?' And he told me, no, he did not," Cotton remembered.

Cotton thought of the composite drawing when he saw the inmate. The inmate's name was Bobby Poole, and he was in for rape. He started working in the prison kitchen too. "The stewards were calling me Poole instead of Cotton," Cotton said. People were mistaking the two men.

Then a fellow inmate told him he'd heard Bobby Poole admit to raping Jennifer Thompson and the other woman that night. Ronald Cotton won a new trial and his lawyers called Bobby Poole to the stand with Thompson sitting right there. It was the moment Cotton had been hoping for.

When looking at Bobby Poole and Ron cotton in the court room, Thompson later said, "As a matter of fact, the strongest emotion I felt was anger at the defense because I thought, 'How dare you. How dare you question me? How dare you try to paint me as someone who could possibly have forgotten what my rapist looked like, I mean, the one person you would never forget. How dare you.'"

Ronald Cotton was convicted again, this time given two life sentences. When the judge asked if he had anything he wanted to say, he stunned the courtroom by asking permission to sing a song. "Decisions I could no longer make. Because my future's so unknown to me. And that I could no longer take," Cotton sang.

Seven more years went by, and then everyone in Central Prison was riveted by a big news story: the trial of O.J. Simpson. "I would get my radio and put my earplugs in, and go outside, and sit in a corner," Cotton said. There, he'd listen to the trial. He was intrigued by something he'd never heard of: DNA. He wrote to his new attorney, law professor Rich Rosen. Rosen warned him that there probably wasn't any evidence left to test, and if there was, DNA could cut both ways. "Understand if the DNA comes back and shows that you did this crime, whatever legal issues we have don't make any bit of difference. You're gonna spend the rest of your life in prison," Rosen said.

Packed away on the shelves of the Burlington Police Department was 10-year-old evidence from the two rapes that night. Inside one of the rape kits was a fragment of a single sperm with viable DNA. It proved what Ronald Cotton had been saying all along - that he was innocent, and that the rapist was Bobby Poole. Within days, Cotton was back in court, this time, to be released. He was filled with gratitude.

In the years since Cotton's conviction, Jennifer Thompson had married and had children. Detective Gauldin broke the news to her. "Her reaction: 'No, that can't be true. It's not possible.' I know Ronald Cotton raped me. There's no question in my mind.'" Gauldin said Thompson cried and broke down. "I mean, she took it all on herself, you know, the guilt, you know, 'I did this to that man'"

But when she thought or dreamed about that night, it was still Cotton's face she saw. To get past it, she asked if he would meet with her at a local church. "I remember him walking into the church. And I physically could not stand up," Thompson recalled. "I started to cry immediately. And I looked at him, and I said, 'Ron, if I spent every second of every minute of every hour for the rest of my life telling you how sorry I am, it wouldn't come close to how my heart feels. I'm so sorry.' And Ronald just leaned down, he took my hands...and he looked at me, he said, 'I forgive you'" Thompson remembered.

"I told her, 'Jennifer, I forgive you. I don't want you to look over your shoulder. I just want us to be happy and move on in life,'" Cotton recalled. "The minute he forgave me, it's like my heart physically started to heal. And I thought,

'This is what grace and mercy is all about. This is what they teach you in church that none of us ever get.' And here was this man that I had hated. I mean, I used to pray every day of my life during those eleven years that he would die. That he would be raped in prison and someone would kill him in prison. That was my prayer to God. And here was this man who with grace and mercy just forgave me," Thompson said. "How wrong I was, and how good he is."

Today, Jennifer Thompson and Ron Cotton are the best of friends. They travel around the world together speaking about wrongful convictions as part of the Innocence Project. [1] This story exemplifies the power of gratitude to invoke forgiveness, compassion and Supreme Love.

The Ship Ramdas Story

There was a man who traveled to my Guru's ashram in Ganeshpuri, located in the south of India. The man lived and worked in the North of India and had to travel several days by train to reach a port, where he traveled the rest of the distance by boat. He had secured a round trip ticket on the ship Ramdas. The man spent two weeks in the company of my Guru at his Ganeshpuri ashram. When the two weeks was up, the man had Baba's Darshan and Baba sent him off with a gift and a blessing.

When the man stepped outside the ashram to hail a taxi, he was arrested by gurkas (Indian police) and taken to the local police precinct for questioning. A woman had been mugged in front of the ashram and the woman identified him as the mugger. The police held the man for two days while interrogating him. They finally let him go after determining that he was not the mugger. By then the man had missed the boat departure on the ship Ramdas for his journey back home.

The man was angry with Baba. He returned to the ashram and demanded to speak to Gurudev privately. When Baba met with the man, the man began screaming at Baba; "I come here for peace and blessings and now look at what I left with! I was arrested and harassed in jail for two days and I missed my ship home. Now I will miss work and they will fire me upon my return. How is this Grace!?"

Baba looked at the man and then told his attendant to fetch the morning paper. When the attendant handed the paper to Baba he showed the front page to the man. The headline read "Good ship Ramdas sinks in ocean. No survivors." The man began crying, realizing that the entire incident with the police kept him from getting on a sinking ship on which he would have died. He gave thanks to Baba and to God.

Steps to Cultivating Gratitude

Gratitude is essential to purify and open the heart. And a pure, open heart is the foundation for the experience of Supreme Love. With this experience you begin to live in a state of Grace.

Gratitude flows easily when you are humble and reverent. So, the steps to cultivating gratitude are the steps to increase your humility, reverence and longing for God.

Humility is a state of Grace, born of Equality Consciousness and steeped in Awe.

To be humble, the complete recognition of Grace is required. The recognition of Grace is the right understanding that nothing here belongs to us. Everything in this world of forms is ephemeral, transient. We come into this world by ourselves and we leave the same way. The body is on loan to us. And whatever we acquire here, while embodied, we have to leave here. We didn't bring any of it with us and we can't take any of it with us.

Therefore, Humility is the realization of how impermanent, how temporary and fleeting life in this world of objects is. This realization brings the understanding and experience that God alone exists – that the nature of the Shiva-Shakti power stomps out all belief in a separate world. When remembered, this awareness of how fleeting life is leaves us in the experience of Humility and Reverence for that One who gives us our time here while embodied.

In this way, Humility is also a reminder that we don't own anything that is on this stage on which we have climbed, temporarily. This is the recognition of Grace, and this recognition must be present for the experience of Humility to be imbibed. Humility is borne of Equality Consciousness. Equality Consciousness is the constant remembrance that the Self, the Supreme Principle exists equally in all – that you are neither greater or lesser than anything or anyone else. You are equal. You respect yourself because you respect the Self and all others as that same One God. As your experience that God alone exists grows and grows, you become steeped in a state of awe, an experience of wonder at God's play as this world and in this world.

Humility is cultivated in the following way:

- By company we rise and by company we fall. So, keep the company of holy beings and those people who are humble and wise.
- Practice making and keeping your restless mind quiet so that you can expand your experience of the indescribable Joy of the Self, your God nature. The vastness of that experience will make you humble. This can be accomplished through daily meditation, chanting, japa and prayer, as instructed by a Siddha Guru.
- Cultivate compassion, love and kindness toward others, even when boundaries to relating have to be drawn. See God in each other in this way.
- Put a check on your ego and your limiting desires and cravings for, as these expand, humility is destroyed.
- Engage in selfless service to others, either in your community or in the ashram of a Siddha Guru. Selfless service purifies the heart and the mind, brings great Joy and increases humility.

Reverence is cultivated primarily by keeping the company of Siddhas and by engaging in daily spiritual practice to experience the Bliss, the indescribable Joy of the Self. Then the limitation of the ego must be addressed by way of the leadership of a Siddha Guru. When the ego is present, there can be no reverence for God. The ego is your false identification with being just the mind, the body and the senses with a given name and upbringing. This ego must be discarded for reverence to take hold. This is a matter of breaking your habit of reaching for the ego by engaging in a daily spiritual practice instructed by a Siddha Guru, and by following the leadership of such a being.

When I first met my Guru, I was engaged as a professional violinist and composer in the music field. My entire identity was caught up in being an artist and I wanted everyone to recognize me and address me as such.

One day my Guru asked me to play along with a morning chant that was offered every day in the ashram. I was given a seat next to my Gurudev's chair and I began playing the notes of the chant as people chanted. However, due to my identifying with being a violin soloist, I began playing quite loudly, as if the chant was my violin solo.

During one morning chanting program, a swami approached me and told me, "Play softly. This is a chant, not a violin concert." Well, I was pretty miffed. So, I ignored the comment and made no adjustment to my playing. A few minutes later, two hall attendants came to where I was sitting while the chant was still going. They told me to get up and follow them. At that time there were bleachers in the back of the meditation hall and they told me to sit behind those bleachers where I could play my heart out without interfering with the chanting. I was insulted!

I stopped playing, grabbed my things and went back to my room. I began packing all my things to leave the ashram. I was fuming. How dare the Guru invite me to play in a chant, only to allow for my complete and utter humiliation! A friend who was in the same room as me had followed me back to the room. He explained to me that Baba was just working on my ego and that I should calm down and return to the chant. So, I did, but without my violin.

For a week I attended the morning chant without my violin. I sat in the back of the Hall, so as not to be noticed. One morning when Baba entered the Hall for the start of the chant, he beckoned to me to come to his chair. Then he leaned over and asked me where my violin was. So, the next morning, I decided I would bring my violin to play for the morning chant. I decided to arrive at the entrance to the Hall before they opened the doors so that I had time to get situated in my seat next to Baba's chair down front.

When I arrived at the Hall doors, I heard a violin being tuned inside the Hall. When I went in to my seat, I found another violinist sitting in it. I told her, "This is my seat," at which point a swami told me that she had been assigned to play the chant with me. She then told me that I could take a seat next to where she was sitting. I was annoyed. Baba entered the Hall and took his seat in his chair. He then leaned over to me, smiled and said, "Play like her, softly." Well, I got through it and continued to play properly for the morning chants.

By way of this episode, my Guru had humbled me. In the months to come I began contemplating my false identification with being just a person, just an individual, just a violinist. By my Gurudev's instruction and leadership, I began to let go of my ego. I began to experience the Joy in being non-attached and this was very freeing. As a result, I became very grateful and that gratitude increased in me over time. Thank you Lord for another day to glorify you!

From the cultivation of Humility and Reverence comes a burning longing to be free. This longing grows and grows over time, by way of Bhakti – devotion to God and to the Guru. It is this longing to attain the freedom of oneness with the Self that eclipses the petty desires and cravings of worldliness. Then gratitude is secured on a permanent basis. From that gratitude Supreme Love is known. Humility, Reverence and Longing are the pillars of Love.

Purity of Mind
and Purity of Feeling

Purity of mind and purity of feeling are essential to the experience of what Love is. I have found that some people are disturbed by the word 'purity' and references or statements to becoming pure. It seems that purity frightens people. If you're frightened by purity or it makes you uncomfortable, this is your ego talking. And, perhaps, you haven't considered what purity really is.

Purity has nothing to do with being a nun, monk or swami. It is not an indication of the necessity to join any spiritual or religious order. It has nothing to do with running away from the world and disappearing into a cave or far off village.

Purity is a state of mind. As your mind becomes less restless, you become pure. When the mind is quiet, the experience of the Self, your God nature shines forth automatically. As you begin to taste the nectar of Self-awareness in this way, your desire for the experience of the Bliss of the Self increases. This is purity. As the desire for the Bliss of the Self increases, you become more and more aware of the vast difference between a restless mind and a quiet mind, and you naturally come to understand that a quiet mind is much more desirable.

As your restless mind becomes consistently quiet with more and more contact with the indescribable Joy of the Self, your desire for the notions and distractions of worldliness decreases. This is purity. This is why here in Nityananda Shaktipat Yoga we say purity is a state of mind. So, purity of mind is attained first by bringing the restless mind under your management, then by directing your restless mind inside to the Self. The spiritual practices already indicated earlier in this book are the means to directing the mind back inside to the Self.

As you do so consistently, you will begin to notice that, even if your mind still wanders, you don't like the impure places that it wanders to. This will increase the desire in you for a pure mind. With practice, your spiritual witnessing awareness will become strong enough for you to observe all of those places that your mind wanders into that you know it should not be allowed to go. At this point, your desire to reign in the restless mind begins to increase. And this will secure for you the understanding of how important it is to engage in a daily spiritual practice for making and keeping the mind quiet. With such a practice, your mind will gradually become more and more pure, meaning free of the distractions and thinking that cause you to contract into the prison of the impurities.

Some of these impurities are anger, worry, anxiety, doubt, fear, loathing, sarcasm and cynicism. What's wrong with being free of these!?

The Play of the Gunas and the Malas

Nityananda Shaktipat Yoga has as its foundation many of the principles and practices of Shaivism, as practiced by the Siddha Gurus of our lineage. Shaivism recognizes the existence of impurities within all of us that must be rooted out if the experience of Joy, Peace and Love is to be attained. As an example, sprinters use the 'obstacles' of weight training, running exercises that include leaps and stretches, jumping hurdles and other barriers in order to make their bodies strong enough to increase their running ability. Similarly, these impurities are said to be 'planted' within us to drive us back to oneness with God by putting forth the effort to root them out. In this way, we become stronger in our spiritual attainment and experience of what Love is.

These impurities are known as the Gunas and the Malas. They are the pillars of contraction that keep God concealed from you. There are three Gunas and three Malas. The three Gunas are Tamas, Rajas and Sattva. Each has qualities that indicate their existence in your being. *Tama guna* gives rise to dullness, darkness, inertia, procrastination, general laziness and a taste for evil thoughts and behavior. These are some of the qualities of Tamas.

Raja guna gives rise to the desire to achieve in order to be recognized as having become somebody. Rajas pushes you to want to manipulate and control outcomes in order to possess people, places and things on some level. This is doership connected to egoism.

Sattva guna, the highest of the three, is that which causes you to want more of a direct, personal relationship with God. It also drives you to want to support ethics, morality and justice. However, there is still doership, as in egoism indelibly caught up in Sattva. People become proud of these qualities and will even argue over the nature of them. For example, spiritual or religious people will argue over which religion or spiritual path is the best or the only one that is recognized as being true. In this way, although Sattva guna is a necessary goal in the early stages of the spiritual journey, even Sattva guna can become a prison and must be risen above.

The presence of these three Gunas in your being gives rise to the three Malas. They are Anava mala, Mayiya mala and Karma mala.

Anava mala is that which gives you the sense that you are just the mind, the body and the senses with a given name. This mala can also cause you to feel ordinary or delightfully weird. With this mala you identify with being just a person, just an individual with very limited agency. If not arrested, Anava mala gives rise to Mayiya mala.

Mayiya mala is that impurity that causes you to feel that you are unique and set apart from everything and everyone else on the planet. It also causes you to believe that duality and diversity are real. If not arrested, Mayiya mala gives rise to Karma mala.

Karma mala is that which compels you to doership. It gives you the feeling that you have the right to possess people, places and things on some level, and that your existence is tied up in how well you are able to do so. This is egoism.

In order to develop the courage to Love and to experience what Love really is, the gunas and the malas must be rooted out. This cannot be accomplished without the Grace, Blessings and leadership of a really good Guru. This is why I took a Guru and began performing the daily spiritual practices he instructed.

Human beings learn best by example. And it is the excellent example my Guru set in having attained to Supreme Love, by way of becoming pure, that became the pillar of leadership for me. Then there was his excellent leadership, wisdom and tests that caused the limitation of my ego to be destroyed, by way of the destruction of the malas and the ability to rise above the influence of the three gunas. In this way I came to experience the supremacy of Love. All my bartering and trading in relationships came to an end. My desire to control was obliterated and only happiness and freedom remained.

Just as a good doctor closely monitors the patient's illness, making adjustments to treatment as necessary, in the same way it is not possible to root out the play of the gunas and the malas without the expert leadership and tests of a Siddha Guru. Testing is necessary so that you always know the difference between where you think you are at and where you are really at in your progress to purity.

Purity of Feeling

Earlier in this chapter, I discussed purity of mind and its necessity. In Chapter 1, I discussed the principle and practice of The Arc. You may want to review that now. Emotions can be very powerful drivers of thinking. Some emotions cause the mind to become more restless and contracted. For this reason purity of feeling is a necessity in the journey to Love. Are you enjoying your senses or are your senses enjoying you? Are you the master of your emotions or a slave to them?

In our Yoga, we recognize the necessity for expressing our humanity. This expression is a powerful spiritual tool when understood properly from the upper story of the inner Self.

The challenge is to be able to express our humanity without becoming a slave to that expression.

For example, it is entirely possible to express anger without becoming a slave to anger – meaning without allowing that expression to impact your inner state. If you are a parent, it is likely that you have already experienced this. There may have been a time when your children were not behaving properly. You may have firmly corrected them. But they ignored the correction, so you had to up the intensity of your demand. Inwardly, you were smiling and did not really want to yell, but you knew it was the next step. So, you raised your voice, feigning anger, to get the children to behave. If, as a parent, you've had this experience, then you know what it's like to express your humanity without becoming a slave to it. In Nityananda Shaktipat Yoga, the instructed spiritual practices are designed to get you to a place where your inner state of Joy is not disturbed by the expression of your humanity, regardless of the emotion expressed.

How To Cultivate Purity of Mind and Purity of Feeling

Purity of mind and purity of feeling are best cultivated by first engaging in Meditation as the observer to increase your spiritual witnessing awareness, also known as Witness Consciousness. This practice has already been discussed in Chapters 1 and 2. We call it Witness Consciousness Centering and it is an easy means of observing all the places that you allow you mind to roam into, where it shouldn't be going. Engaging this practice increases your understanding of the urgency for daily Meditation, Chanting and Japa. These practices have also been discussed earlier in this book.

As you engage in these spiritual practices on a daily basis, your restless mind will become more and more quiet, allowing for the direct experience of the Bliss of the Self on a steady basis. Over time, your growing experience of the indescribable Joy of the Self will cause your mind to become pure. The necessity for daily spiritual practice in this way can never be over emphasized.

The next step is to engage the practice of The Arc. The principle and practice of The Arc was offered in Chapter 1. This practice is very effective in freeing you from slavery to emotions, while allowing you to express your humanity freely.

Without purity of mind and purity of feeling it is impossible to know and experience what Love is.

Love for Love's Sake Alone

All the Love you give is really meant for you. In spiritual life, the giving of unconditional Love automatically reveals God. In this way, the purification of the heart is inevitable. Loving for Love's sake alone renders great Joy and makes you humble and reverent.

The great sage Yajna Valkya was asked by his wife to tell her how Love endures. Yajna Valkya said that the secret to Love is in understanding that a person loves another not for the other person's sake, but for his/her own sake. This is so true. When you Love with this understanding, without wanting to possess outcomes, you elevate yourself to the abode of the true heart. Then you become a better lover, a better friend and companion.

In this regard, Shri Rumi has a wonderful aphorism.

THIS WORLD WHICH IS MADE
OF OUR LOVE FOR EMPTINESS

"Praise to the emptiness that blanks out existence. Existence: this place made from our love for that emptiness!
Yet somehow comes emptiness, this existence goes. Praise to that happening, over and over!

For years I pulled my own existence out of emptiness. Then one swoop, one swing of the arm, that work is over.
Free of who I was, free of presence, free of

dangerous fear, hope, free of mountainous
wanting.

The here-and-now mountain is a tiny piece of a
piece of straw blown off into emptiness.

These words I'm saying so much begin to lose
meaning: existence, emptiness, mountain, straw:
words and what they try to say swept out the
window, down the slant of the roof." [1]

The emptiness Rumi speaks of is a mind
empty of thoughts, notions and limiting desires
and craving. This is a silent mind, the experience
of which allows Love to blaze forth
spontaneously with the indescribable Joy of the
Self. In that Joy everything worthwhile takes
place and Love is automatically known. In
another of his writings titled *No Expectations*,
Rumi tells us:

"A spirit lives in this world
and does not wear the shirt of love,
such an existence is a deep disgrace.

Be foolishly in love,
because love is all there is.

There is no way into presence,
except through a love exchange.

If someone asks, But what is love?
Answer, Dissolving the will.

True freedom comes to those who have escaped
the questions of free will and fate.

Love is an emperor.
The two worlds play across him.
He barely notices their tumbling game.

Love and lover live in eternity.
Other desires are substitutes for that way of
being.

How long do you lay embracing a corpse?
Love rather the soul, which cannot be held.

Anything born in spring dies in fall,
but love is not seasonal.

With wine pressed from grapes,
expect a hangover.

But this path has no expectations.
You are uneasy riding in the body?
Dismount. Travel lighter.
Wings will be given.

Be clear like a mirror reflecting nothing.
Be clear of pictures
and worry that comes with images.

Gaze into what is not ashamed
or afraid of any truth.

Contain all human faces in your own
without any judgment of them.

Be pure emptiness.
What is inside that, you ask?
Silence is all I can say.

Lovers have some secrets that they keep." [2]

And in the Bhakti Sutras of Shri Narada, in verse 54, we are told:

"This supreme love is devoid of attributes; it is free from all selfish desires; it grows in intensity every moment; it is an unbroken inner experience, subtler than the subtlest." [3]

Attachment Brings Suffering

Attachment always brings suffering. This is true of all relating and can be closely observed in the most intimate of relationships you choose to be in. Attachment is an ego expression that compels you to want to possess people, places and things to some degree. It increases your desire to manipulate, possess and control outcomes. In this way, attachment always diminishes the ability to Love and the experience of the supremacy of Love. There is no freedom through attachment.

We all want to be free and everyone wants to be happy. The challenge is that most people look for freedom and happiness where they are not. In Nityananda Shaktipat Yoga we are inspired to the Truth about freedom and happiness through the understanding of what Love is and where/how it is to be found. Love is freedom and happiness is a direct result of being free. So, freedom is found through Love which is Supreme due to its unconditional nature.

That unconditional nature is God's Love that is inherent in the inner experiences of Peace and Joy. When you drown in the currents of that indescribable Joy you begin to realize that you are Love – that your very nature is that Love boat.

Rumi tells us "A thousand half-loves must be forsaken to take one whole heart home." [4] Indeed, to experience the supremacy of Love, you have to forsake all of the ways in which you mistake satisfaction for Love. You have to set your ego aside and seek to be fully present in the moment with loving for love's sake alone. For this to happen you really do have to come to know your God nature.

There Is Right, There Is Wrong and Then There is Love

Do you want to be right or do you want to be blessed? Because you can't be both. The experience of what Love is takes you beyond notions of right and wrong, good and bad. In another poem Rumi states:

"Out beyond ideas of wrongdoing
and rightdoing there is a field.
I'll meet you there.

When the soul lies down in that grass,
the world is too full to talk about." [5]

Love is not a particular action or expression. Love is an inner state of being from which springs wisdom and joy. These arise out of direct contact with the Bliss of the Self and your direct experience that you are That.

As I have shared previously, the understandings you reach for and embrace will determine whether or not you are able to experience the supremacy of Love and whether

or not you will embrace the courage to Love.
Should the understandings you reach for and
embrace about Love come from those who have
not experienced its supremacy, or from those
who have merged in it? This is a question I asked
myself often after keeping the company of my
Guru and experiencing his Love. The
observations I made by way of this experience
helped me to understand the very nature of Love
and its purest expression.

Years ago we had our place in Queens. I
was offering programs in a large room above a
row of shops in Woodside and I lived in a nearby
apartment building. One evening I had been
invited to offer a program at a healing center in
Manhattan. After the program, I headed back
home. On the way back, as I was driving along
Queens boulevard, my Guru appeared to me
inwardly and told me to take a right at a certain
stop light, which I did. I was told to keep driving
to the end of that street and then to take a left,
which I did. The street I was on came to a dead
end at a topless bar.

Gurudev told me to go into that bar – that
there was someone inside who needed to be
rescued. I hesitated at first. I was wearing my
saffron program robe. I thought to myself, "What
am I doing here!? Suppose someone who
recognizes me sees me going into this topless
bar? Then I will be the headline on the late
edition of the evening news!" Well, that thought
took about thirty seconds. Then I got out of my
car and entered the bar.

I was directed to go past the bar and find
a door in the back, to the left. As I moved in that
direction, a bouncer followed me. I found a dark
corner with a door that was ajar. I quickly
entered the room to find a nude woman with a

syringe hanging from her arm. She was almost unconscious. I removed the syringe from her arm, picked her up and quickly carried her out of the bar.

After placing her in my car, I asked her where she lived. As it turned out, she lived about 5 minutes away in an apartment with her brother. I took her home and helped her into her apartment. By this time she had come to enough to be able to speak. Her brother was out at work and we had a conversation about her demise.

She told me that she was from Ireland and lived with her parents. She had run away from home and wound up living with her brother in Queens. He got her the job dancing at the topless bar and also turned her on to drugs. She had progressed to heroin and also had become an alcoholic. I asked if she wanted to get off drugs and alcohol. She told me she did and I recommended that she get into a local rehab program.

At that point we meditated together and she received Shaktipat from this one. I stayed with her a while and then left. About 7 months later I ran into her at a local restaurant. She looked very different and told me that she had gotten into a rehab program. She was off drugs, clean, and was almost sober and off alcohol. We spoke about her returning to Ireland and she indicated that she wanted to but had no money or resources to get back. She was also concerned that her parents would not take her back, given the circumstances under which she ran away.

I happened to know an Irish Catholic priest who was affiliated with a local church. I introduced her to him and he contacted her parents and then arranged for her trip back to Ireland, paid for by the church. What Grace!

Is Supreme Love Too Lofty An Ideal?

It is because people have the skewed understanding that love is an ideal that they are not able to experience what love is. Love is not an ideal or notion. I remind you again that Love is an inner experience of an active, Divine principle and energy. The Self-Realized Love Beings of our lineage all say, "In the beginning, Love is somewhat tainted, somewhat selfish." But any Love is better than no Love. Even if the Love is tainted in the beginning, you start there. In other words, you start with whatever capacity you have to Love. It may not be that you have a great capacity to Love. Your capacity to Love may be very small in the beginning but you start there.

Here in Nityananda Shaktipat Yoga, we teach methods and we also embrace the wisdom understandings of the great sages of our lineage. With respect to these understandings and methods taught, we've seen, over a period of many years, that people are able to gradually express Love with fewer and fewer conditions. They are able to gradually express Love in ways that are more and more supreme, meaning more and more unconditional. That happens first, by way of people recognizing that God exists in them. That has to be the first recognition.

For true Self-love, you have to recognize that you are a Divine Being, even with all of your foibles and perceived mistakes. You have to recognize God within yourself. We teach methods here for doing that. As you begin to experience that it's true—that God exists within you as you, as you begin to have that experience, you develop the desire to express Love in a more unconditional way, and that happens gradually over time.

Here's something else that happens: People who are able to express Supreme Love are better lovers, they are better friends. As you begin to expand your ability to Love in the way I've described, you become a better lover, a better friend. You begin to attract to you far greater relationships. As you journey through your interactions and have those experiences, you then develop a stronger and stronger desire to Love others unconditionally because you see God in them.

It's a gradual process, but we've seen people here completely transformed over time. You don't have to be a Saint, you don't have to be completely pure. You can begin right where you are. Your intention is a very powerful thing. Your intention to expand your experience of Love, your intention to Love yourself first, more completely, as God, as the Self, is a very powerful tool. As you nurture that intention you can gradually— and it may not happen in a week or ten days or even several months; it may take several years – but you can gradually expand the way you're able to experience and express Love unconditionally.

As you observe your own expansion in this regard, you gain a great deal of joy and peace. As you begin to have more and more experiences of Love, Joy and Peace in this way, you want to then Love in a more unconditional fashion. It's gradual, but Supreme Love, and the ability to express it, becomes automatic as your experience of the Self grows.

As you heighten your experience of the indescribable Joy of the Self, by calming the restless mind, by making the mind silent, by dissolving the mind when you don't have to be engaged in any tasks, as you experience that Joy welling up inside you, it becomes very easy to take the step to love unconditionally, *even when you have to draw boundaries.*

So, it's a gradual process, but we've seen it happen here. I've seen it happen over and over and over again with people who are far from being saints. I know it from my own experience in the early stages of my own Sadhana when I was anything but a saint. So, it's entirely possible. In this regard, strong leadership is essential.

I am so grateful that I had the incredible leadership of my own Shri Gurudev in this regard. This is why we have Nityananda Shaktipat Yoga, and this is why we have the leadership that Kedarji extends, and the profound leadership of the Siddhas of our lineage, of which there are many. This is why this leadership exists. With leadership by example, it becomes very easy to take the steps to begin to understand that Supreme Love, indeed, is not a lofty idea, and that it can be attained by everyone, even you.

The Secret To Intimate Relating

Shri Rumi has a wonderful aphorism about the secret to intimacy.

LOVE AND I TALKING

Love says, You cannot deny me. Try.
I say, Yes, you appear out of nowhere
Like the bubbles in wine, here, then not.

Love says, Prisoned in the body-jar,
Singing at the banquet.

I say, This ecstasy is dangerous.

Love says, I sip the delicious day,
Until night takes the cup away.
Then I insist night give it back.
The light I see by never changes.

Arabs describe wine with the word *mudam*,
which means *continual*. On and on and on,
because wine drinkers never get enough.

The water of realization is the wine we mean
where love is the liquid, your body is the flagon.

Grace floods in. The wine's power
breaks the jar. It's happening now.

The water of waking becomes the one who

pours, the wine itself, and every presence at the banquet.

No metaphor can hold this truth.
that knows how to keep secret
and when to show itself. [1]

Friendship

Friendship is the expression of Supreme Love. God is the friend to all. By that example, we can extend friendship to others through loving kindness and respect, even to people who we perceive to be strangers. Loving kindness and respect go a long way and usually have a greater impact than we even know. These naturally lead to the expression of Love in its highest form.

True friends will nurture each other without condition. Friends accept each other for who they are in the moment, not for who they want each other to be. These are basic tenets of friendship that allow Supreme Love to flourish.

With respect to intimate relating, I have observed that the best and most lasting of relationships, including marriages, are always defined by a strong friendship that supersedes the bartering and trading of needs and wants. This kind of relating is a necessity for Love to flow without taint.

THE WATER WHEEL

Stay together, friends.
Don't scatter and sleep.

Our friendship is made of being awake.

The waterwheel accepts water
And turns and gives it away, weeping.

That way it stays in the garden, whereas another
roundness rolls through a dry riverbed looking
for what it thinks it wants.

Stay here, quivering with each moment
Like a drop of mercury. [2]

An important key to friendship is the
ability to be fully present in the moment with
relating and the expression of Love. The first
step in being fully present in the moment is to be
fully present with the Self, your highest nature,
in the present moment and from moment to
moment. A strong, daily spiritual practice is the
means to this experience. When you are able to
be fully present in the moment with God, you
develop the ability to be fully present in each and
every moment of interacting in friendship.

Years ago my friends were popular with
me, but I grew less and less popular with them.
At one point several of these friends pointed out
to me that I always appeared to be 'somewhere
else' while in their company. While interacting
they would ask, "Where are you right now?" This
is because my mind was, typically, somewhere
else while I was interacting with them.

It wasn't until I met my Guru and engaged
his leadership that I was able to break this habit
by being fully present with myself, the Self, first.
As I reined in my restless mind and stopped it
from wandering all over town, I was able to
experience the precious gems that the present
moment holds. As a result, it became easier for

me to be fully present in the moment in my interactions with others.

Friendship means seeing God in each other and offering Love and Respect based on that. Here in Nityananda Shakipat Yoga we refer to this as Equality Consciousness – a term my Shri Gurudev used often. Equality Consciousness is a state in which there is no sense of duality left in you and no sense of separateness from God and from others either. It is a state where you bask in DIVINE unconditional Love for God and others and this Love has no expectation whatsoever. This experience gives rise to humility and reverence for God and humanity.

Don't Label It

There are many labels for relating, especially where intimate relationships are concerned. "Boyfriend," "girlfriend," "husband," "wife," "lover," "significant other," "soulmate," "life partner," and so on. With these come a host of understandings, many of which are not very useful for relating. These understandings are often heaped upon us by others and by the acceptance of societal norms that have become the superimposition of the masses. In this way, these labels can be a hindrance to sharing and experiencing the supremacy of Love.

For example, the word "intimate" that is used in the title of this chapter has a host of understandings connected to it that are, often, accepted connotations that people don't examine closely. For example, for many years during my adulthood I understood intimacy as meaning sex or 'love-making.' And I found that this understanding was common among the people I knew and interacted with. The fact is you can have intimacy without sex, something I later learned and enjoyed as a result of my spiritual growth. In fact, any love exchange involves intimacy.

Years ago I lived in a five story apartment building in Queens. An elderly widow lived in the apartment above me. She had no carpets on her floors and whenever she walked around her apartment there was a huge thumping sound that came through the ceiling of my apartment.

One day I decided to knock on her door to talk to her about the noise. She opened her door cheerfully and introduced herself as Mrs. Bliss. Well, what an introduction! After introducing myself, she told me about her condition and the passing of her husband. She had problems with her feet and wore special shoes to address the issue. These were the only shoes she was able to wear and the shoes were thick and heavy. She also had problems with her legs that made it difficult for her to walk any distance.

After explaining this to me she handed me a shopping list and asked if I would get the items for her. I couldn't say no, so I went shopping for Mrs. Bliss. At this point, I had not yet told her why I knocked on her door. This occurred several times, with me knocking on her door, intending to speak to her about the noise, and her handing me a shopping list of items she needed.

Several weeks later, as I delivered her groceries, she turned to me and asked, "Why did you knock on my door the first time you came up here?" I explained to her the issue with the thumping noise every time she moved around in her apartment. She apologized for the noise and I asked her if she would consider carpeting her floors to dull the sound. She agreed to do so if I would make the arrangements and supervise the install, which I did. During the course of these events we had become the best of friends, enjoying the intimacy and supremacy of Love.

So, how can labels interfere with sharing what Love is? Labels often lead to objectification. People view each other as mere objects of sense and shape their relating around others being an object of their desire on some level, to some degree. This is connected to limiting desire and craving that people feel others exist in their lives to fulfill.

For example, a husband with a physically beautiful wife may see her as an object of his desire for sexual fulfillment or vice versa. Another seeking companionship may see an intimate friend or lover as having the duty to make him/her happy. A manager of a sales department may see the sales team as machines hired to churn out sales and may see potential customers as mere dollar signs.

A pharmaceutical company may view the side effects of its products as an opportunity to sell more products to treat those side effects rather than improving on the side effects themselves, in this case viewing patients as part of its business model for financial growth.

All objectification of human beings is connected to the *fulfillment of expectations*, another challenge with respect to labeling in Love exchanges. Because, with labeling comes more and more expectations of outcomes that breed more and more objectification. Since the supremacy of Love rests in its unconditionality, expectations and objectification are barriers to loving because they give rise to conditions in relating that are connected to objectification.

Here it is important to remember that having expectations and engaging in objectification are acts that prevent you from being fully present in the moment with your God nature (the Self) and the same God nature of others. In other words, these prevent you from seeing God in yourself and others – a prerequisite for the experience of the supremacy of Love.

Years ago I was married. I had not yet fully committed to taking up the spiritual practice instructed by my Guru. In this marriage, both myself and my wife at that time (eventually we divorced) were caught up in some of the standard labels connected to 'being married.' There were a lot of expectations about sexual performance and frequency. Then there were the expectations that being married meant having children. There was a lot of pressure in the marriage to immediately begin planning for when we would have children.

Then there were notions connected to 'being married' that created expectations about being seen together as much as possible when interacting with family and friends. We wanted to appear as 'an item,' simply because we were married. There were also a lot of expectations around ending certain friendships with people we both had been intimate with (even without sex having taken place), due to our understanding that 'marriage' meant there could be no intimacy that might supersede the intimacy of the marriage in any way. In other words, due to labeling, we both felt that loving each other meant there were other people in our lives whom we could no longer share intimacy with on any level.

In this way, over time the marriage lost its spontaneity and became more and more 'mechanical,' with more and more having to be planned out in advance. Due to labeling, there were also expectations about who was supposed to pay the bulk of the bills and manage the finances. Eventually, the marriage became a chore to maintain because there were so many expectations to meet, and less and less of them that were being met.

Labeling and Lack of Communication

Because labeling often leads to expectations, it also creates assumptions about what should and should not take place. And, in general, assumptions lead to a lack of direct, open and honest communication. Lack of direct, open and honest communication is a major cause of breakdowns in relating.

Assumptions also create understandings that usually are not useful for interacting. I remind you of the principle and practice of *The Arc* that was discussed in Chapter 1. The understandings you reach for and embrace are everything with respect to experiencing the supremacy of Love. Understandings that are tainted due to assumptions will always lead to feelings and the expression of emotions that hinder a Love exchange. As such, without direct, open and honest communication the supremacy of Love cannot be experienced.

So, how is not labeling the relationship different than setting boundaries? Boundaries are set in order to command respect in relating, by way of invoking a change in behavior. Since setting boundaries requires direct, open and honest communication, the act of doing so is an act of Love because the supremacy of Love cannot be experienced without mutual respect.

Keep An Open Heart

Loving one person does not mean not loving another. Depending on the type and quality of the interaction boundaries have to be set. We choose to interact differently with a friend than we would with a lover, husband or wife. These boundaries actually support our ability to Love all unconditionally while recognizing and experiencing the supremacy of Love.

This happens when we keep an open heart and insist on being fearless in all our interactions. In this way it is easy to experience that loving one person does not mean withholding Love from another.

Growing Apart and Moving On

It is common for people engaged in relationships of varying degrees of intimacy to grow apart. This happens in marriages as well. The fact is, over time, people take on different pursuits, their interests change and, in many cases, they realize that what they thought they wanted they no longer want. Others have changing needs that will not be met in the relationship. And there are times when people simply decide that the relationship is over, regardless of the level of intimacy. In some cases, the relationship is simply no longer a priority.

Sometimes growing apart means changing the boundaries of the relating. At other times it means ending the relationship altogether. The above are all observations and choices that can and should be made.

After meeting my Guru and experiencing Shaktipat and his spiritual leadership, my vision and experience of my existence here changed dramatically. I quickly realized that I had become a different person, a better person, and that most of the relationships I had chosen to be in were no longer the company I wanted to keep. There were people I hung out with, engaged in activities that I was no longer interested in pursuing. Since those relationships were founded on those activities, I no longer had any desire to maintain them and I ended them.

Then there was my live-in girlfriend. Our relationship became strained when I chose to spend time in the company of my Guru and those people I had met in his spiritual community. It wasn't that I had stopped loving her. However, gradually, I lost interest in many of the activities we engaged in together. I was changing and growing, and my girlfriend had little interest in my spiritual growth or attainment, and even less interest in hearing about it.

So, we quickly grew apart. I told her that there were things in our relating that she wanted that I could no longer give her. I also told her that, if she wanted those things, she should have them by finding someone else who could give them to her. She moved out and found another boyfriend. We remained friends but the boundaries had changed and this was fine with both of us. I never stopped loving her and, eventually, we both moved on. Even then we stayed in touch with each other from time to time, until she married and moved out of the country. Later, I was married and the marriage ended in a similar way.

These are some examples I can give from my own experience. There is nothing wrong with growing apart and this is not a fault of anyone engaged in the relating. It is a fact that most human beings do grow and change in varying degrees, and at different paces. And some don't change at all. When it comes time to change the boundaries of your relating with others, or when it comes time to move on, do not be afraid to do so. There is no shame or guilt in this.

Such things are a fact of life and it is entirely possible to change boundaries or end the relating without any loss of Love. This is so because Love is an inner spiritual principle and experience that is not dependent on anything or anyone outside yourself. Love is who you are. If you remember this, you will have no problem with moving on when having grown apart in any relationship. And you are not responsible for how the other person feels when you make such choices. You are only responsible for how you feel.

To see God's Grace and Love in everything, from a blade of grass to a speck of dirt. This is Love.

Love is the bridge between you and everything.

The heart that drinks from the cup of love remains ecstatic forever.

Love is an ocean of Grace that transforms you from the inside out.

Love is all there is.

Love for Love's sake alone.

See God In Each Other

My Guru used to say, "See God in each other" and this became his emblematic instruction. When we see each other as God, that vision paves the way for us to respect and uphold human dignity by refusing to see each other as an object of desire to manipulate and possess. In this way, we are able to treat and Love each other as human beings, without condition, even when boundaries need to be drawn to command respect.

The objectification of others is the expansion of egoism that destroys the experience of Love. We are raised to pass ourselves off as objects of other people's desires and to see others as objects of our own desires. Many years ago this was my conditioning. For example, I saw women as objects of my desire and craving and pursued relationships with this notion. In addition, women pursued me with the same understanding and contracted notion. This led to intimate relationships and a marriage in which there was a lot of bartering and trading of needs for wants. In this way, much of the relating became a 'business deal' and Love took a back seat to the management of this trading. As a result, in the end, these relationships did not last.

All of this changed when I met my Guru. Through the blessing of his spiritual leadership and Grace I came to understand and experience that true friendship is the key to relating in the experience of the supremacy of Love.

Ocean of Love

Sri Rumi writes of Love in the following way:

Ocean Love

God is pleased when your love realizes
It is part of something oceanic
And begins to move with the whole.

The larger love is more real,
Being itself reality. These forms, a mix
of earth and water. Yes, you say,
but I already have a deep love.

Not deep or vast enough.
More like riverwater filled with silt.
Don't wash your hands there.

The love you must enter lives in the saints
and prophets. It is already the ocean, whereas
most loving still filters through countryside,
enjoying the passage.

The ocean says, Quit *pretending* to be clear.
That pretense keeps you from receiving
What I can give.

Your water wants to reach the sea,
but landscape keeps holding it back.

If you could shake lose your foot,
the earth would be completely dry
and ocean water completely free.

But desserts and undiluted wine
soak you back into wet ground.

Wanting wealth, power, and more tasty food
Have made you drunk.

When you can't have what you want, you get
headaches.
That hungover disappointment is proof
That what made you drunk was desire.

Let a more measured necessity
govern the intensity of wanting.

You say, I don't need help with this.
I am already united with God.

That's like groundwater claiming to move with
the tide.
Not yet. Stay with those who have pure love.

The taste of milk and honey is not it.
Love instead that which gave deliciousness.

This world is a watery shadow of ocean-love.
The sea of light cannot be contained
in single human beings, so leave fragments,
and be the mountain.

As you become existence,
you will distribute creation,
lavishly blessing everybody.

Hold out your apron to catch what comes
with being in the presence.

Don't tear the cloth collecting stone.
Wait for the smooth old coins,

the silver and the gold.

Don't *pretend* like children
that rocks are precious.

Let the held-out apron be your honesty,
and don't worry about finding a white-haired
teacher.

Merging with ocean-love has nothing to do with
age or the color of anyone's hair. [1]

Great Respect

My Guru used to open every one of his
talks and discussions by saying, "With great
respect and love, I welcome you with all my
heart." When we see God in each other, this great
respect is automatic and becomes easy to
nurture and experience over and over again.
Respect is the hallmark of any love exchange. It
is the measure by which we know that we are
experiencing love. This respect comes from the
direct experience of God within our own being,
the foundation for which is our growing, direct
experience of the indescribable Joy of the Self.
Tasting this nectar, this Bliss of the Self
comes with spiritual practice that is engaged on
a daily basis, first to rein in the restless mind and
then to go beyond the mind and the senses to
that witness to your mind. That witness, that
indweller is who you really are. From that
witness to your mind you are able to observe
this appearance of a world as a play of the Shakti
that is produced and directed by God's Love.

This daily spiritual practice is something that is instructed by one who has drowned in that Love and gotten across. Such beings are Siddha Gurus with the ability to awaken the dormant spiritual witnessing awareness (kundalini) in you. These beings also have the power and ability to lead you on the journey to Supreme Love.

Love God

Loving your God nature is loving God. You and God are already one. You just need a growing and ongoing experience of this fact.

In his Bhakti Sutras, Shri Narada tells us the following in verse 65:

"Dedicate all your actions to God and direct all your passions, such as lust, anger, pride, and so forth, toward God." [2]

A profound way to experience that you are Love and that Love is all there is, is to make all your daily activity a blessed sacrament to God. This is done by perfecting all your activity, no matter how small or seemingly insignificant, with one-pointedness of mind. You can lose yourself in activities in this way while remembering God and the Guru. This is a very good way to become absorbed in the supremacy of Love while going about your daily, mundane activities. Remember, you are Love.

In addition, there is a wonderful contemplation that you can perform in this regard. It goes like this:

*I, who am an embodied being, endowed with
intellect, life breath, and their functions, now offer
up all my actions and their fruits to the fire of
Brahman. No matter what I may have done, said
or thought, in waking, in dreaming, or in
dreamless sleep, with my mind, my tongue, my
hands, or my other members; May all this be an
offering to God.*

Love is the bridge between you and
everything. The heart that drinks from the cup of
love remains ecstatic forever. Love is all there is.

I experience all of this that I have shared with
you by the Love, Grace and Blessings of my Guru.
I end this work with an offering of praise to him.

By Your Love I Am

Where You Are I Am

Where I Am You Are

In Flowers, Trees, Grass and Water I Am

In Roots and Fibers and Dirt and Wind I Am

When You See Me, You Are What Is Seen

When I See You, I Am What Is Seen

By Your Love I Am Omniscient, Omnipotent and
Omnipresent

Sun and Moon Am I

Tracing My Own Steps Across the Sky

Appearing and Disappearing In a Single Breath

Welling Up In Space and Time

By Your Grace, I Am the Revealer and the
Revealed

Residing In Being Be

All That Is Comes to Complete Rest In Me

My Devotion to You Has Turned Me From a
Beggar to a King

By Your Love I Am

**Drown in the Ocean of Love
May All Be Joyful**

References

Chapter 4

1. The Innocence Project; https://innocenceproject.org/.

Chapter 6

1. Shri Rumi, translation by Coleman Banks, The Essential Rumi, HarperOne Publishing, ISBN 978-0-06-250959-8, pgs. 21-22.
2. Shri Rumi, translation by Coleman Banks, Bridge to the Soul, ISBN 978-0-06-133816-8, pg. 76.
3. Shri Narada, translation and commentary by Swami Prabhavananda, Narada's Way of Divine Love, Vedanta Press, ISBN 0-87481-054-X, pg. 125.
4. Shri Rumi, translation by Raficq Abdulla, Words of Paradise: Selected Poems of Rumi, ISBN 10: 0711226512 ISBN 13: 9780711226517.

Chapter 7

1. Shri Rumi, translation by Coleman Banks, The Essential Rumi, HarperOne Publishing, ISBN 978-0-06-250959-8, pg. 354.
2. Shri Rumi, translation by Coleman Banks, The Essential Rumi, HarperOne Publishing, ISBN 978-0-06-250959-8, pgs. 247-248.

Chapter 8

1. Shri Rumi, translation by Coleman Banks, The Essential Rumi, HarperOne Publishing, ISBN 978-0-06-250959-8, pg. 354.
2. Shri Narada, translation and commentary by Swami Prabhavananda, Narada's Way of Divine Love, Vedanta Press, ISBN 0-87481-054-X, pg. 136.

About Kedarji

Kedarji is the Founder of The Bhakta School of Transformation, an Ohio-based not-for-profit public charity devoted to lasting Inner Peace and permanent spiritual transformation. The curriculum offering here is based on Kedaji's 4 Pillars of Joy In Daily Living.

He had an early career in the Performing Arts as an actor and singer in Broadway musicals, plays, movies and television. He went on to study violin and conducting at the Juilliard School of Music and graduated with degrees in performance and composition from the Manhattan School of Music. Later, he studied Eastern and Oriental Medicine, graduated with degrees in both from the Kushi Institute, and had a practice in New York City for many years.

Leading With Love

Kedarji helps people embrace the Grace in life's joys and challenges in a way that causes lasting happiness and peace. In a world seemingly mad with greed and corruption, Kedarji has a long track record of helping people affirm and expand the best parts of their lives.

He is a Sadhu in the lineage of the great sage and saint, Bhagawan Nityananda of Ganeshpuri. He imparts the same instruction and leadership he was taught— the same methods used by a line of spiritually proven and powerful masters who have uplifted people's lives for thousands of years.

A Sadhu is one who has made the commitment to live as an ascetic, renouncing the pursuit of worldly pleasures and fantasies to serve the greater good and to work to uplift humanity. In this regard, Kedarji is also known as a Sadguru, meaning true spiritual leader, and a Shaktipat Guru (see below) who leads by example in becoming both wise and well with a powerful, heart-centered approach.

Practical Leadership In A Shaktipat Guru

Kedarji has a reputation for leading without insisting that people follow. This allows students and seekers to come to our approach in their own way. For Kedarji, the reference to Sadguru is a reference to our lineage of Siddha Gurus on whose shoulders he stands and takes refuge in. This is the great Shiva lineage that Bhagawan Nityananda of Ganeshpuri also made, of which Kedarji is a part.

Wise, Happy and Well

Many of Kedarji's students say that, through his leadership, he has transformed their lives in profound ways not experienced in other modalities or on other paths.

His students blossom and uncover hidden strengths through a well-integrated and time-tested approach. Through his leadership, it's possible for anyone and everyone to experience life's magic in a way that they come to know their true nature and attain a state of lasting happiness, peace and joy.

With his 4 Pillars of Joy In Daily Living as the foundation (the Spiritual Power, Improved Mental State, Emotional Resilience and Vibrant Health), he combines the power of Grace of his spiritual lineage with the time-honored, Siddha Science of the Yoga of the Siddhas. This powerful combination includes his skill as a Shaktipat Meditation master.

Authentic Shaktipat Guru – Shaktipat Meditation Master

Kedarji is a Shaktipat Guru. He has been vested with the power and authority to fully awaken and nurture the dormant spiritual awareness known as Kundalini. Specifically, this awakening occurs by way of the transmission of the Grace-bestowing power inherent in the Blessing of Shaktipat. In particular, you will find that Kedarji is a recognized and very skilled spiritual leader and Shaktipat Meditation Master. Additionally, his is the ability to lead you on the journey to the realization of your true nature or Self-Realization. Indeed, this is a journey in which you retrace your steps back to God.

Author/Producer

Kedarji is the author of several books and courses, including:

- Vibration of Divine Consciousness. A Spiritual Autobiography.
- The Verses On Witness Consciousness.
- The Abode of Grace - Bhagawan Nityananda of Ganeshpuri.

- How To Be Fearless, Happy and Resilient In The Age of Noise and Distractions (a video home-study course and weekend retreat).
- The Sutras On The 5-Fold Act of Divine Consciousness.
- Dharma and the Preservation of Liberty.
- Live Strong and Be Happy. Learn The Daily Rituals of The Most Spiritually-Powerful, Happiest and Healthiest People On The Planet.

Spiritual Journey

Kedarji began his quest to understand and fully imbibe Yoga Science at an early age. Feeling incomplete, Kedarji began an intense spiritual journey that took him to India and Asia. Soon after, he experienced an initiation, an awakening into the power of true Meditation, Chanting and Contemplation that formed the foundation for putting all the pieces together.

Due to this event and ongoing application of the methods taught connected to it, Kedarji was able to fully apply the science behind well-being that is based on the Spiritual Power. He calls it the energy substratum of everything. His direct, unfolding experience of this power is the basis for the integration of his 4 Pillars of Joy In Daily Living embodied in his unique approach: An approach that combines Siddha Science and the science of a holistic lifestyle of health and well-being with the transmission of Grace that he extends as a God-realized, Shaktipat Guru.

About Nityananda Shaktipat Yoga

Love is the highest religion, the greatest spiritual path of humankind. Therefore, we welcome you with Love, we Honor you and we Respect you. In addition, our path of worship and study is led by Kedarji. He is a Sadguru (meaning true spiritual leader), holistic practitioner/researcher and natural healing scientist who has a reputation for leading without insisting that people follow. To this end, here you will experience programs that embody worship through meditation, chanting, prayer, contemplation and the study of scriptures/sacred texts. We are a non-denominational sanctuary of worship open to people of all paths and faiths.

For more information about programs, events, courses and retreats to strengthen the practices and awareness spoken of in this book visit

NityanandaShaktipatYoga.Org